# I want a **Divorce?**

Simone E Katzenberg is an experienced solicitor specialising in family and divorce law. She was born in South Africa but now lives in London and is an active member of the Solicitors' Family Law Association and the Family Mediators Association. After she spoke on Talk Radio over 300 listeners rang in to request any material she had published on divorce. This is her first book.

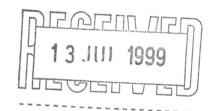

Reviwed
7th Sept 2000

# I want a Divorce?

First published in Great Britain in 1999 by
Kyle Cathie Limited
20 Vauxhall Bridge Road
London SW1V 2SA

ISBN 1 85626 321 5

Text © 1999 Simone E Katzenberg
Editor: Kate Oldfield
Copy editor: Robina Pelham Burne
Editorial assistant: Sheila Boniface
Typesetting: Heidi Baker

Simone E Katzenberg is hereby identified as the author of this work in accordance with Section 77 of the Copyright, Designs and Patents Act 1988

A CIP catalogue record for this title is available from the British Library

Printed and bound in Singapore by Kyodo Printing Co. Pte. Ltd.

# Contents

# Foreword

Divorce is an emotive subject, and not only for those who are going through it. In 1996, when the Family Law Act was being debated in Parliament, a war of words was waged in the press and on television and radio. Passionately held views about 'family values' and the abolition of 'fault-based divorce' caused arguments as fiery as any between a disputing husband and wife. Then and now Relate, with sixty years' experience of counselling couples with relationship difficulties, keenly supported the fundamental concept enshrined in the Act: that the adversarial nature of divorce does harm – to couples and their children and ultimately to society.

We know the conflict is damaging. Finding ways of minimising conflict in divorce is difficult, but not impossible, and this remarkable book makes a huge contribution to the cause. Simone Katzenberg speaks to her readers with wisdom, compassion and patience born of long experience working with men and women who have contemplated and gone through the devastation that is divorce.

The seven stages of divorce do not constitute a neat formula of the author's devising; they mirror the sequence of painful emotional states which she has observed at first hand. She describes with deep understanding the powerful feelings which affect everyone – the break-up of a marriage is a great leveller – as the bonds of attachment are broken. As Relate counsellors work to help clients explore and understand what is happening in their lives before making the decision to act, so Ms Katzenberg seeks to provide the insight and information that make it possible to survive divorce, pick up the pieces and start again.

People find life changes difficult and distressing – changes that are actively sought, like getting married, a new job or a house move, those that are almost certain to happen at some time or another, like the birth of a child, illness in the family, death, and those they hoped would never happen: divorce and separation predominate in that category. Learning to accept that the ups and downs of life are normal makes it much easier to cope with them. By the same token, accepting that tumultuous emotional states are a normal part of going through a divorce enables people to manage that process more effectively. This book offers that reassurance, and demonstrates a sensitive appreciation of the role the relationship counsellor can play.

Simone Katzenberg builds a bridge between the private suffering of individuals and their children and the public stage upon which divorce proceedings take place. While explaining the legal implications with great clarity, she also offers sensible advice about using solicitors' skills to best advantage. At a time when people are in turmoil, the down-to-earth counsel of this book will feel like a breath of fresh air: 'say what you feel before it's too late – it's not a time to be proud'; 'try with all honesty to put the children first'. Case studies reinforce the author's strong case for children to be protected from the worst excesses of adult revenge (indeed the section on rage and revenge should be compulsory reading for the helping professions too). Divorcing parents are likely to experience times when their needs are in conflict with those of their children and in truth will find it very hard to find ways of serving both at every stage of the process. But this book appeals to adults in the grip of primitive emotions to use their will to overcome the desire to punish their partner, to take courage and keep in touch with their responsibilities as parents. Furthermore it offers a map of parenting while divorcing that will help to identify the particular issues which may become the focus of counselling.

It is unusual to find a book where considerations of the emotional and the practical so effectively inform each other. It will be invaluable not only for people contemplating separation, separating or going through a divorce, but also for their friends, relations, GPs, solicitors and counsellors.

Sarah Bowler
Chief Executive, RELATE

# I want a divorce
## ... or do I?

Do you? Perhaps you do, but the prospect is very frightening and you do not know where to turn, whom to speak to, how to go about it. Questions are building up in your head, consuming your every waking moment, and if you don't find answers, you think your head will explode. Perhaps you are adopting a more ostrich-like approach – if you pretend that it is not happening, it will all go away, and one day you will wake up to find it was just a dream and a bad one at that.

You may be somewhere between the two: not terribly happy, just finding life rather dull as you trundle along from day to day waiting for some life-changing event or person to transport you from mundane suburbia to an exotic, carefree, happiness-filled existence.

Or you may have met someone else and are one of those people who march into a solicitor's office and say: 'I want it to be quick. I want it to be cheap. I want it to be amicable.' But it is not that simple. Whether the divorce will be quick, cheap and amicable has in fact very little to do with solicitors. In reality, you are lucky if even one of these aims is achieved. For the work of the solicitor is only a small part of the process which leads to divorce. The other part, the emotional part, is more difficult.

Whoever you are and however you feel, if you are reading this book you are either thinking of separation or in the process of separation. Indecision pervades your thoughts and moves, and your mind is filled with questions which need to be answered before you can make the decision which will so profoundly affect your future and which needs to be taken with thought and care.

It is important that when you do make this decision you are in the right frame of mind, that you have had the opportunity to think it through and have taken legal advice. Whatever you do, do not let anyone rush you or make decisions for you.

This book is unique because it links the emotional aspects of a separation with the legal elements. This book is aimed at everyone who is considering or is in the process of a separation and/or divorce, whether they are living together or are legally married – the emotional fallout is the same.

However, for those who have not married but cohabit, Section Two, which deals with the legal implications of separation, is relevant in the following respects:

Insofar as financial matters are concerned, at present the law provides little in the way of protection or guidelines for unmarried couples. A person's rights over property are governed by the Trusts of Land and Appointment of Trustees Act 1996 which is explained in the chapter entitled: The Beginning.

All the sections which deal with one's relationship with solicitors and barristers as well as illustrating court procedures are applicable to everyone reading this book.

The sections which deal with parental rights over children are applicable to married and unmarried couples alike.

Resolution, especially amicable resolution, of a separation or divorce is dictated almost entirely by the emotional elements. I believe there are seven stages to divorce, seven emotional stages that everyone will experience, irrespective of age, gender, race, cultural background or profession. No one is immune to the huge impact of divorce on one's self-esteem and well-being. That is what this book is all about. Although your head tells you to be sensible, practical and realistic, your heart reacts emotionally; you experience waves of intense emotion over which you have little or no control.

The emotional stages which I have identified are as follows: breakdown; shock; anger; pain; hatred; grief and, finally, acceptance. Until both of you have worked through the various emotional stages in your own time, you will find that it is simply not possible to negotiate settlements or finalise legal proceedings. The legal side of divorce is so intricately linked with the emotional aspect that they can only be considered in conjunction.

Until you have acknowledged and passed through the stages, and are really ready to let go of the relationship, the divorce itself, the financial settlement and arrangements for the children will not be resolved. Agreements will be sabotaged, one or both of you will move goalposts and unimaginable frustration will overwhelm you.

But, given time, these issues can be resolved and you will emerge from the process able to start your life again. It is a tunnel through which everyone travels whether it has been a short or long relationship and whether you are the one who wants the separation/divorce or not.

You may well wonder how it is that I am able to make these statements with such certainty and conviction. For the last seventeen years, I have practised as a family solicitor and mediator. I spend most of my working days unravelling the complicated lives of others, coaxing them through the process, and then waving them off to begin a new life when the legalities of the separation or divorce have been completed.

The material for this book is based on my observations of my clients and their partners behaving in a particular way at a particular time. Identifying the seven stages and documenting how clients have reacted during the stages has shown a pattern of behaviour which is exhibited by everyone, irrespective of personal circumstances. Their behaviour is a mystery even to themselves.

It was after a harrowing day during which I had no fewer than four telephone calls from clients whom I was representing, demanding that financial offers which they had made be withdrawn, threatening to liquidate their companies and leave the country or just to give up work, that it struck me that these four were all experiencing the same feelings. I realised that everyone goes through the same emotional stages: everyone, from all walks of life, men and women alike, experiences the seven stages of divorce.

My analysis of the seven stages may provide you with the impetus to make your relationship work, if that is what you want. If you decide to separate after all, my explanation of the seven stages will sustain you as you move down the path ahead.

Everyone goes through the same process. As in childbirth, the pain and emotional upheaval of divorce know no boundaries; regardless of status, colour or creed, all are hurt. Setting out the various stages is helpful for a number of reasons:

- It is important to realise when you go through the general hiccups of a long-term relationship that a separation or divorce is not a soft option and should never be a first option. By being aware of just how difficult it will be, you can consider whether there is an alternative or a way in which to save a relationship rather than bail out when the going gets tough.

- If you feel that the choice is not even yours and that separation and ultimately divorce are inevitable, it is important to have an understanding of the emotional stages that you will go through. You will then know what to expect and understand that the feelings which you experience are unavoidable and are part of the process. At those times when you feel down and vulnerable, it is reassuring to know that everyone has the same feelings.

- Lastly, knowledge will provide hope: hope that however low you may feel, whatever anguish you experience, just when you feel that you cannot take it any longer, it does all end. You will survive it and you will be able to start life afresh.

Through this book I hope that you will find the strength to get through each and every stage, knowing that each stage is but a phase, a phase that will in time pass. And as each stage passes, it draws you closer to the final stage of acceptance, the point at which you are able to let go of the past and the hurt and move on.

I hope that in reading this book, you will gain an understanding of why you are feeling or reacting in a particular way at a particular time. This will help you adapt and control your responses, which will give you both a short-term and a long-term advantage.

Read this book before you start the process and again as you go through the stages. Read it when you feel despair, anger, sadness. Read it to identify the stage you are at, knowing that the feelings you have are no different from those most people in the same position feel. Read it when you feel dragged down by it all and be reassured that your feelings are just part of the process, a process which you must go through in order to deal with the separation or divorce in a healthy way. Read the book knowing that however terrible you feel, it is one of the stages and you will eventually get through it.

Read it when you are halfway through the process, too far down the road really to turn back, but close enough to know that the end of the divorce is in sight. You will be able to see just how far you have gone and how much closer you are getting to the final stage of acceptance. Feel reassured that you have somehow managed to get through some of the stages, and believe that you will manage to get through the rest. Read it and know that when your solicitor tells you at the outset what the stages are which you will go through, that this is exactly what is happening. But most of all be reassured that eventually this phase of your life will come to an end and you will be able to move on.

I have found that those people who do not acknowledge their emotions along the way tend to become emotionally stuck. They become bitter and cynical, and the whole process becomes unbelievably more complicated and more difficult to resolve. Dealing with the emotional side of a separation within the same time frame as the legal process ensures that by the time the legalities are concluded, you will in all probability have resolved the emotional elements and truly be able to move on.

The key to it all is timing – it will take as long as it takes and no one can predict how long that will be for you. What I have found is that those who deal with their fears and other emotions through counselling or something similar are the ones who move on more quickly. Placing your feelings in a little box and shelving them, pretending that it is not happening or that it is happening but it is not your fault and has nothing to do with you, tends to prolong the process and delay the healing. It will be that much longer before you are free from the past and ready to take on the future.

What I have learned from my clients is that the majority of people find a surprising inner strength. They have had to fight for survival in times of enormous distress and, in doing so, overcome obstacles which they had never even considered. Having had the privilege of being so close to so many brave people, I have been able to share their experiences and transpose them into a format to encourage others during similar adversity. You too can do it: you too can survive and you too can start life again. So many of my clients have proved that there is indeed life after a separation and/or divorce.

As a solicitor, I feel strongly that the decision to separate is a very personal one, to be made only by the couple involved. What has been expressed again and again by many of my clients is that divorce is not a soft option. By the same token, many have reached the conclusion that to be alone is still preferable to being locked into a bad marriage, one in which there is no prospect of resolving the difficulties.

Always remind yourself that this is your life, your relationship, your marriage and perhaps now your divorce. You are the one who must decide what it is that you want, and the course of action you will take. And if in doubt, don't do anything in a hurry, but wait until you feel ready.

For each stage, I will identify the characteristics of that stage, explain what you can expect, advise what you can and should not do, and, if there are children, explain how your emotions or the emotions of your partner when experiencing any of the stages can impact on the children. Being able to identify not only the way in which you feel but also the stage which your partner has reached, will help you understand your respective responses to situations.

During the legal process, you will be experiencing one of the emotions described in Section One. Ways in which to cope with the emotional stages when they impact on the legal process are discussed in Section Two, in which lawyers, procedures and courts are also explained.

Statistics indicate that divorce is more likely if you marry younger than twenty-one, your parents divorced, you live together before marriage or if one or both of you is in a second marriage. Divorce is always in the news; the public is intrigued by the failing relationships of the rich and famous. People identify with the human suffering in these circumstances. And somehow it makes it all more bearable that even they can feel the pain, anger and all the other emotions, .

Britain still has one of the highest marriage rates in Europe but it also has the highest divorce rate. With some 350,000 people divorcing per year in the United Kingdom alone, there is a constant stream of people entering the arena of the breakdown of a relationship. Recent statistics show that one in three marriages will end in divorce and this is rapidly rising. It is predicted that 4 out of 10 new marriages are likely to end in divorce and that second and subsequent marriages have an increased risk of failing.

Statistics also show that those couples who live together before they marry have a higher risk of divorce than those who marry first. And for all those couples who opt for cohabitation rather than marriage, their relationship is just as likely to disintegrate within the first five to nine years, at the same trigger points, as for married couples, when for example one reaches the age of thirty, forty or fifty or when the children leave home. There are also countless people who feel a general dissatisfaction with their relationship but are not sure whether to embark on the road to divorce. So if you fall into any one of these categories, feel reassured that you are not alone.

And always remember, when the going gets tough and you feel it is unbearable, when you are filled with uncertainty and indecision,

> **No matter how hard it all seems**
> **No matter how long it all takes**
> **Be strong,**
> **have hope,**
> **it does all end.**

# Section One:

## the seven stages

# The seven stages

By the time you read this, you will already be in stage one of the seven stages of separation. Before I go on, let me reassure you that being on the first rung, so to speak, does not in any way mean that your relationship is doomed and that you are destined for the divorce courts. What it does mean, however, is that your relationship is experiencing difficulties, difficulties which, if not acknowledged and dealt with, may lead you or your partner to the conclusion that your relationship cannot be saved. If you still care, and if you care enough to try to do something about it, then you should take steps to confront the problems and attempt to and find workable solutions to them.

Many people enter the first stage and never venture further. Their relationship survives or perhaps even thrives on the cycle of turmoil, devastation, reconciliation and turmoil again. Others find that, despite the apparent collapse of their relationship, they genuinely do not want it to end and will stay together, albeit unhappily, for the rest of their lives. Others will seek the reasons for the breakdown and work successfully with the assistance of counselling towards a reconciliation. This may lead to a better and closer relationship because each has made a conscious and renewed decision that they do, after all, want to stay together. You must do whatever feels right and whatever works for you irrespective of what others may say.

In reality, however bad you think the whole separation and divorce will be, it is likely to be worse than anticipated and that is even if you have both reached an amicable and mutual decision to separate. But there may be no alternative. You may feel you have no choice but to go ahead with a divorce. Perhaps your partner is the one who is determined to end the marriage and the choice is therefore not even yours. It is always difficult to disentangle when you have shared an important and intimate part of your life with another. It takes time and understanding and there is no short cut.

If your first port of call in the event of a marital crisis is an experienced family solicitor, you will not be frog-marched willy-nilly through an acrimonious divorce. On the contrary, you will be asked a lot of questions about what it is that you want. If there is any chance of repairing your relationship, and this is a route which you want to follow and one in which your partner is willing to participate, then you will be encouraged to so do by attending couple counselling.

There will be times during the process of divorce when you will experience intense and, at times, uncontrollable emotions. You will be angry, angry with your solicitor because you think it is all taking too long and costing too much, and angry with your partner for delaying it all and trying, you believe, to squeeze you dry, both emotionally and financially.

You will feel hurt, ashamed and uncertain, torn apart by your love for your children, the lost love of your partner and the apparent hopelessness of the situation. You will feel like throwing up your hands and running away, not caring whom you hurt on the way, and then caring so much that it hurts until you physically ache. You may threaten to put your company into liquidation, leave the country and disappear. You will cry, man and woman alike – tears of sadness for what you have lost, of nostalgia for the past when you were once together and happy, and tears of frustration over how it has all turned out.

## Children

During the breakdown of a relationship, the subsequent separation and finally divorce, one or both parents will have to cope on a day-to-day basis not only with their own feelings, but also with those of their children. The children are, after all, the truly innocent victims of a relationship which breaks down. The children are the reason why parents will remain in contact and bound together long after the dust has settled in relation to the divorce. The children are the ones whom parents should try their utmost to protect from the devastation which an acrimonious divorce can wreak. It will at times be unbelievably difficult.

As parents, you will both need to work very hard towards a common goal: to protect the children as much as possible from the potential ravages of divorce. It will require a great amount of effort on the part of both of you. The reward will be well-adjusted and balanced children; children who will be able to move freely between both parents, enjoying quality time with each, and who can make the most out of having two homes.

Children in divorce need to be nurtured and protected more than ever, and by *both* parents if possible. They need to know that, despite the fact that the marriage is breaking down or has broken down, both parents still love them. They need to know that their parents are divorcing each other, not divorcing themselves from the children. They need to know that by showing love for one parent, they are not betraying the other. They need to know that they can continue to love both parents openly without each parent competing for more love. And the only way in which this can be achieved is through encouragement and reassurance from both parents.

But how do you do this when your partner is, for example, demanding contact with the children but refusing to pay maintenance, or is flaunting his or her new partner whilst you suffer the pain and effects of the breakdown? Or when your partner constantly blocks any attempts to retain an ongoing relationship with your children, in effect sabotaging all your efforts to see and maintain a relationship with them? What you really want to avoid is your children being caught in the middle of a tug-of-war in which no one wins or achieves anything.

This is where an understanding of the various emotional stages can help to clarify what is happening and why. It will enable you to understand why you and/or your partner are reacting in the way in which you are. Such an understanding can help you through what is often a long and frustrating process, both emotionally and legally, without dragging your children along with you in self-destruct mode.

Reassurance that you are not alone, are not inadequate, are not failing to cope, and that what you are feeling is part of the process, is intended to give hope, to enable you to survive the course and move on. One client wrote to me, 'My own brain cells and decision-making capabilities appear to be on hold, and my emotions vacillate between anger, frustration, guilt, sadness and total numbness. Had I not known from you that this was normal, I might have thought I was going mad.'

If you are a parent, you need to be constantly aware of the effect that your behaviour or reaction to a situation will have on the children. Thoughtless or vindictive behaviour towards your partner can rebound, often unintentionally, on the children. Try to take one day at a time and try to think before you act rather than react in a negative way.

It is easy for others to proffer advice when they are not experiencing the same feelings as you. The children, however, have these feelings too. They are being denied the opportunity of being brought up by both parents together and they too need time to adjust. It does not help them to adjust to changes if there is constant and ferocious conflict between their parents. It is not and must never be a contest over who has more time with the children; the children must not be placed in a position in which they feel that they have to chose one parent over the other. It may be that in order to avoid a battle, one of you may have to be the more 'grown-up' and back off to protect your child from a wrangle. Irrespective of how much it hurts you, you need to make sure that it is not your child who is being hurt by the conflict. And as your children get older, they will respect you and appreciate what you have done to protect them rather than having memories of constant court battles and arguments about contact.

Knowing what to expect and understanding what you are both doing and why, you should both be able to prevent unnecessary friction, and this will benefit the children. If it results in one fewer battle, it must be worthwhile.

In the chapters which follow, I will refer to the various emotional stages which accompany separation and/or divorce. These emotions may not only affect your ability to cope with the children's emotions but also the way in which you and your partner handle certain issues. Difficulties over contact, in particular, tend to ease over time and as the children get older. If you have children, then try to bear in mind the following:

- At any time, you may be experiencing shock, anger, pain, hatred or grief;

- Particular emotions cause you to behave or react in a particular way, examples of which are set out in each chapter;

- Try to see how the children are feeling and try to channel the situation in a more positive way for both the children and yourself.

At each stage of the process, step back and try to separate the way you feel towards each other from the way you feel towards your children. Question the motive behind your actions and try with all honesty to put the children first, doing what is right for them even if it does not necessarily feel right for you or satisfy your needs.

Examples are set out below of some of the things that parents do to each other and the children during these difficult times. By being conscious of what you are doing, you can try to control behaviour when a similar situation arises again. Sometimes parents become so embroiled in a cycle of behaviour that they feel unable to stop or simply do not want to stop for fear of being thought weak, for fear of giving in or for fear of the other parent taunting them that they have won!

Divorce is not a game – there can be no winners. Try to refrain from using the children as pawns, otherwise resentment may fester in your children, leading to untold problems. No matter how badly you may think of each other, the denigration of one another, either to the children or in front of them, can only make things worse for them. After all, they did not choose their parents, but you chose each other.

The children cannot have other parents and the words 'for better or worse', which applied to the two of you when you married, now apply only to the children. It is up to you as parents to make it better for them, not worse; you will always remain their 'mum' and 'dad' and no one can take that away from you or them. You need to make sure that you do not destroy that unconditional love that children give to their parents, a love that needs to be preserved more than ever after separation, irrespective of the obstacles your partner may place in your way. The children will always need to know you still love them however hard that may be for you. At times it may feel easier to walk away, but your children will never understand why and may find that they are not able to forgive you for something they can't understand.

Most people will pass through the seven stages and start again, afresh. They will have survived, many with a strength of character they did not know they possessed. Some survive, but bitter, scared and cynical. Through counselling and other help, they too can emerge, not unscathed but stronger, strong enough to start again with new hope.

# Breakdown

## The causes and timing

The stage of 'breakdown' has the most variable time span, in some cases months, in others years; generally it tends to develop over a long period of time. Through pressures of work, children, different goals, dreams, ambitions, you drift apart. You lose interest in each other, are constantly under stress and frequently cannot even be bothered to talk to each other. You may find that you stop sleeping together and the intimacy you once shared ceases. You may find that you row endlessly or don't talk at all to each other for days at a time. You stop caring whether or not the other takes sugar in coffee or find that mentally you switch off as soon as the other starts talking to you so that you hear nothing of what is said, your mind wandering, somewhere far away in a fantasy of your ideal world.

Slowly but surely this lack of communication erodes the very basis of your relationship. Unless either one or both of you acknowledges what is happening, you will find that your life together, is no longer bearable and the strain of maintaining the facade of unity starts to take its toll.

You or your partner feels the need to 'escape', and ways in which to do so consume your thoughts. But what do you do? And when? You may find that there are just too many days when you feel that you live like lodgers in the same house with separate lives, slowly but surely drifting further away from each other. The catalyst will often be an affair or one argument too many. It exposes the general dissatisfaction with your relationship. This may for the first time precipitate discussion about the 'D' word, a word too difficult to verbalise yet constantly on the tip of your tongue and on your mind. You are terrified to think about it, frightened to articulate it, yet you feel the inevitability of it creeping upon you.

The breakdown of a relationship can be long and tortuous or sharp and swift, or anywhere in between. It never just happens overnight; some couples live together in a state of semi-breakdown forever and never do anything about it. Not every relationship can be saved and not everyone wants to save or salvage what is left of theirs. You may wish that you had separated years ago rather than enduring an unhappy marriage for so long. Everyone goes through the emotional stages of disentangling, however, and you may, without being aware of it, have already gone through some of them by the time you read this and before you approach a solicitor or counsellor.

Lack of communication, differences in opinion, lifestyle or interests also erode the basis of a relationship. If you are unable to draw strength from each other, unable to conquer your difficulties, unable to fulfil each other's needs and expectations, breakdown sets in and starts to tear you apart. But who does what and when?

When Joe first came to see me, he was distraught that his wife of thirty-two years was about to divorce him. He told me that he had been a good husband, didn't fool around with other women, didn't drink, didn't beat her and worked hard to maintain a comfortable lifestyle. He did not understand what had gone wrong and why, out of the blue, she wanted a divorce. He was just beginning the breakdown stage.

Gloria, on the other hand, wanted to separate from her husband of twenty-seven years because she had been unhappy for the past twenty years. She told me that her husband did not listen to her; he was generally too busy with work and golf and she felt that she might as well be on her own now that the children had left home. And when she told her husband, he was as surprised as Joe was.

Michèle has a husband who has been a philanderer from the first year of their marriage. Every year or so she comes to see me to discuss a separation, and on three occasions has started divorce proceedings against her husband only to withdraw them when they have reconciled. Last time I heard from her, they were together and very much in love! Michèle drifts in and out of the breakdown stage and her relationship seems to thrive on the post-reconciliation periods.

Billy was beside himself with distress when I first met him. He had only been married for three years, he had a young son and his wife was pregnant by another man. He had had no idea that anything was wrong with his marriage.

All these people are in the breakdown stage. Some of them will remain there for quite a while, even years, whereas Gloria is ready to move on, as she has been contemplating the issues for many years. As for her husband, he is right at the beginning of the process.

## Taking action

Whatever form the breakdown takes, there are always two main questions:

1. Should I see a solicitor?
2. What do we tell the children?

Taking the first step and contacting a solicitor does not and need not sound the death knoll of your marriage. The first meeting with a solicitor is usually a fact-finding exercise. It provides you with an opportunity to ascertain your rights, discuss what to expect and determine the possible outcome. In this way, when you feel ready to make a decision about what to do, you are able to make an informed one. The worst possible thing that anyone can do is act on impulse, without fully thinking through the implications or understanding the consequences. Ensure that your solicitor is a member of the Solicitors' Family Law Association (SFLA), members of which adhere to a code of practice and strive to implement a non-adversarial approach to separation and divorce.

During the breakdown stage there is an enormous amount of uncertainty and the decision to separate and perhaps divorce is an extremely difficult one to make. You will find that you change your mind over and over again. Do not despair: it is quite usual to feel utterly confused. You are about to make a major decision and you want to be as sure as possible that you have explored all the alternatives and that if you do decide to separate and ultimately divorce, it really is the only possible option open to you.

Separation and divorce are quite different. If a couple separate, they usually live separately and apart, but people can separate yet still continue to live in the same house. They will sleep in separate bedrooms, not eat meals together, not go out socially together and to all intents and purposes be considered 'separated'. However, if one of you moves out, then by that act alone you become separated.

There are no automatic legal implications to being separated and if you decide to reconcile, the person who left can simply return home. However, for a divorce, steps must be taken to set in motion a legal process which can take place whether you are separated or not. What is required is the belief by one of you that the marriage has broken down irretrievably. I go into the legal implications in greater depth in Section Two.

## Counselling

It is during this stage that I would recommend that if there is any prospect of resolving your differences and working towards a reconciliation, you try to do so. You are likely to need the help of an independent third party in the form of counselling. Sometimes the point of counselling is to assist you in making the decision whether to separate or not; sometimes it is to work positively towards reconciliation.

You may already be in counselling and there is no reason why you should not continue. This should not interfere with couple or marriage guidance counselling. You can still continue with your individual counselling, which may deal with separate personal problems, whereas marriage guidance deals with the specific difficulties that exist within your relationship.

Ideally, and to preserve your own well-being and inner balance, continue with counselling for as long as you need it and if you do decide to divorce, then continue until the divorce is finalised. You will have good days and bad days and you need to know at all times that there is someone there for you, and you alone, to help restore your equilibrium when it all seems too much to cope with alone. There is no need to struggle on your own – you will not get a medal at the end of the day for being a hero.

Counselling can provide many benefits. Greatest of all is that it affords you the opportunity of talking through your fears and concerns without judgement. Although you need to inform your family and friends of the situation, it is sometimes better not to tell them all the reasons for the breakdown. There are numbers of reasons for this: primarily it is because they will take sides, they will advise you, and they will judge your partner. If your partner has enjoyed a close relationship with your family, it will be difficult for them to maintain this relationship. If you and your partner decide to reconcile, it will be all the more difficult if others know the intricacies of the breakdown, and you may feel that they then judge you in wanting to try again. Although unlikely to have any legal training or background, family and friends may advise you on how to run your case and tell you what to do. If everyone is coming at you with different advice, it will confuse you, and you will not know whom to listen to or where to turn. Stick to the professionals. We know our areas of expertise, we do not judge you and because we are not involved with you, we are able to provide you with proper and sound advice.

## Telling the children

It is usually at this time that you need to tell the children about the breakdown and the burning question arises: how and when to tell them? The breakdown of a relationship is traumatic, and not only is the timing crucial but also, and even more importantly, the way in which the children are told. Speak to those who have received information which has had a devastating effect on their lives and they will tell you that what they remember most clearly is the precise moment at which they heard it. It is at the stage when reconciliation is not a realistic option that the schools need to be informed.

In a perfect world, both parents would be able to approach the subject together in a sensitive, caring and adult way, committed to ensuring that their children are protected from the potential trauma of divorce as much as possible. Unfortunately this tends to be the exception rather than the norm because so often it is just too difficult to cope with your emotions so rationally. Many parents will attend joint counselling specifically to get help in finding the best way to break the news to their children.

Martine and John went to see a couple counsellor specifically to discuss how and when to tell their children about the pending separation and divorce. A weekend was chosen and it was decided that they would tell the children together after they came home from school on Friday. This would give the children the whole weekend to ask questions and they would be there to comfort them. But John returned home late from work on Friday, by which time the children were already in bed and fast asleep. Martine started to fume and they decided that they would tell the children first thing on Saturday morning. However, on Saturday morning, John stayed in bed as long as possible and when he did get up, he promptly left the house, telling Martine he had work to do.

Martine had psyched herself up emotionally to tell the children. She knew that they were conscious of the discord and had to be told, yet the weekend was fast disappearing and John was running away, clearly unable to cope with facing the children. By Sunday afternoon, the children had still not been told and John had successfully avoided the issue. This led to a heated confrontation during which Martine blurted out to him in front of the children, 'Why don't you just tell the children that we are getting divorced?'

Many parents at this stage cannot control their emotions in each other's presence. The children may have been exposed to violence in the marriage. They may have been exposed to frequent tantrums and rages. They may have been emotionally and/or physically abused by one of the parents. In these situations it is not possible for the parents to sit down together and explain their plans to the children.

The situation at home may have been unstable and outwardly hostile for so long that the children realise that it is just a matter of time before one parent goes. That in itself may be a relief to the children as it will put an end to the constant bickering and conflict. Often the uncertainty of the situation may be almost as bad as the decision to part.

In ideal circumstances, you may want to wait a while before you break the news to the children. However, your distress may mean it is not possible to continue putting on a brave front. The children may need to be told sooner rather than later. The fear of the unknown and your unprecedented distraught behaviour may frighten them and be more distressing than the knowledge of why your behaviour has changed so radically.

Whatever the situation at home, there will be enormous sadness for any child, old or young, when faced with the harsh realisation that mum and dad are going to separate. Every child wants their parents to remain together always and this is so even when it is clear that it is not possible. Every child has a dream of a family unit with mum and dad not fighting, loving each other forever and having a secure home.

How and when you tell the children will depend on your own personal circumstances. If you are able to tell the children together, then do so. The children can be assured that even though mum and dad can and will no longer live together, their continued love for the children remains, independent of their feelings for each other. You can all cry together and answer questions that the children may have. Provide as much reassurance as you can that they will be able to see the parent who is leaving. What has happened has nothing to do with them but is between you as adults. Your dual role as parents will continue. It will be the beginning of a period of adjustment for all of you and you will have to take it one step at a time.

The situation is more complicated when you decide to divorce but due to circumstances will not actually separate until either the property in which you all live is sold or the divorce is finalised. The conflict is ever present and your children may bear witness to many emotional confrontations between you as the frustration and hurt of the situation takes hold.

You may be the parent who is left to tell the children without the support of the other parent. It is difficult to have to tell the children on your own, but there may just be no option if your partner will not co-operate or if your relationship is so volatile that you are unable to discuss or talk about anything without a row erupting.

Try to choose a time when no one is in a hurry to get anywhere, no guests are expected, and a favourite television programme is not about to start; wait until homework is complete, then take the telephone off the hook, switch off the mobile, hold each other and talk. Choose the time with care: for example, if a child is about to take exams or a birthday party is imminent, it may be better to wait until after the exams or the party.

It is important to notify the schools of the situation and talk to the children's head teachers in the first instance. The school can give your child any extra attention and support needed and alert you if any difficulties arise as a result of the breakdown. For example, if your son, previously even-tempered and sociable, becomes aggressive and rude, the teacher will understand why. Rather than reprimand him, the teacher can talk to him. This may even open an avenue of communication for your child, so that your child knows that there is someone outside the family to whom he or she can talk.

If you are the parent who leaves the home, notify the school of your change of address. The school can keep you informed of all school activities and functions as well as send you school reports, as extra reports need to be specifically requested. If your relationship has broken down to the extent that you are not talking to each other at all, this step is an important one in order to preserve access to information about the children at school. Generally schools are supportive to children and parents and will send out duplicate notices, reports, etc., to both parents to encourage continued involvement of both of them.

At this stage, when you have made the decision to separate and have told the children, there are certain important points to bear in mind. Firstly, provided you are married to each other, you both have what is called 'parental responsibility'. This is explained in Section Two.

Secondly, neither parent can remove the child from the jurisdiction of the court, which means (permanently) from this country, without either the consent of the other parent or a court order. If you fear that your partner may attempt to remove or abduct your child/ren, you must seek legal advice without delay. In such a situation, speedy action is essential. Retain the children's passports and notify embassies and the Home Office so that no passports are issued without your consent.

## Taking time

This is the longest stage and perhaps the most difficult of all, because it is during this stage that you acknowledge to yourself and then to others that the relationship is breaking down. It is frightening and lonely. You are going to have to make one of the most important decisions of your life. If you are uncertain about what it is that you want or what you should do, consider your options:

- Couple counselling;
- Individual counselling;
- Taking time to reflect and decide.

During this stage my advice is: if in doubt, don't! One day you will wake up and find that you have made the decision, be it to stay together and work it out or that separation is the only option. Take whatever time you need and do not let others rush you.

## Stage 2
# Shock

Facing up to the fact that your relationship has broken down and there is no realistic prospect of reconciling your differences leaves you in a state of shock. As in most traumatic experiences, nothing can prepare you; unless you are in that situation, it is not possible to envisage how you will feel. You may wander around in a daze, become absent-minded and careless and are likely to lurch from one emotion to another and back again. You feel that this cannot really be happening to you. You cry, you scream, you shout, you withdraw at times numb from the shock of realising that this time it may really be over.

The impact of this stage depends on the circumstances. How long has the marriage been unhappy? Was the separation planned or completely unexpected? Obviously, if your partner of twenty years walks in and tells you that he or she has met someone and is leaving, the shock will be enormous. The shock can be just as great if your partner provides no apparent reason and as far as you are aware everything is the way it always has been. There have been threats to leave in the past, but neither of you has left; this time is different and you can't understand why.

## A third party

If there is someone new who has precipitated your decision, it is better to be honest about it. Your partner will then rightly or wrongly lay the blame of the breakdown at the door of the third person, even though you believe that is not necessarily the true reason. Meeting someone may have highlighted for you the problems in your relationship. It has made you realise that you do not want to spend the rest of your life miserable, in what you now feel is a second-rate relationship. It may have given you the courage to take the big step, a step that you have thought about for years. If you don't mention the new person, your partner will agonise over why this time is different from all the other times. Your partner will think or believe that it is all their fault or that they can win you back.

When your partner then discovers the presence of another, there will be feelings of humiliation and shame in addition to the shock. In my experience of cases, I have found that the feelings of anger which then follow are much greater and more vengeful than those when there is openness about a new relationship. The existence of a third person moves the blame away from you, which may not necessarily be right but makes the emotional transition a little easier to bear. Particularly in the initial stages, it is often easier to blame someone else rather than face up to the part that you may have played in the breakdown. In time and with the help of counselling, whether you try to reconcile or not, you will need to go beneath the surface and come to terms with what was really going on in your relationship.

## Counselling and medical help

Out of the blue, the feeling of shock can leave you quite devastated and temporarily frozen into inaction, unable to make even simple decisions or to plan any further than the immediate present. It is a time of enormous turmoil, indecision and fear. During this stage, you may feel desperate to do all you can to make amends, to fix what is wrong, but you simply do not have the energy. You may feel lethargic, exhausted and tearful. You may feel isolated, ashamed and very alone, unable to discuss it with anyone, unable to face the world. Your self-confidence plummets and you may feel that if you tell anyone, they will consider you a failure and reject you.

Perhaps the shock is so great that you eat compulsively or are unable to eat at all; unable to talk about it, you may contemplate ending it all if only to punish your partner. If you feel yourself spiralling downwards, contemplating self-harm, it is essential that you talk to someone, anyone who will help you, support you, and take you to your doctor who can advise and guide you through this stage. It may be necessary for you to go on to anti-depressants for a while, but whatever you do, do not try to struggle through this stage on your own.

> One of my clients, Andy, told me that he had been on Prozac for five years and had no intention of stopping. His doctor told him he could take it forever. I was shocked by this and made enquiries of my own. Both a GP and a psychiatrist to whom I spoke thought this attitude cavalier and irresponsible. Those on prescribed drugs should have counselling as well as anti-depressants, with the prescription of drugs being reviewed on a regular basis. I tried to encourage my client to seek counselling but he initially refused. I suggested that we deal with the divorce, and when it was over, that he work towards coming off the drugs. After the divorce and when he felt more able to cope, he did go to counselling and is now off the Prozac, in a new relationship and moving on with his life, a prospect he never would have thought possible when he first came to see me.

> Another client, Helen, was in a fairly hysterical state when she first came to see me. She told me that she had lost three stone, was unable to stop crying and was not sleeping. I referred her to counselling and her counsellor liaised with her doctor, who gave her anti-depressants to take her through the initial stages, in conjunction with counselling. For Helen the drugs were an essential short-term crutch and no more than a crutch to see her through the early weeks or months, until she could start to surface and focus on what was happening.

If you are in this situation, in time and with the help of counselling you will have to work through your feelings, come to terms with what is happening, come off the drugs and move on with your life. It is essential that if you are prescribed anti-depressants, you see your doctor regularly and do not take them without also having counselling. Crutches are fine in the short term, but when you feel ready to run again, you must be able to throw them away – they must not become a lifelong essential.

The same advice applies if you find yourself becoming dependent on alcohol or involved in compulsive-type behaviour. It is crucial to seek help as early as possible.

You may find that you are constantly replaying the last scene, going over and over in your mind the conversation or event which signified the end of your relationship. Your mind is in turmoil; at times you feel quite out of control. Plans have to be considered, people need to be told, and some decisions do need to be made. What will you do? Where will you go?

What about the children? What about money? How will you do it? Can you do it? All these questions and many more slip in and out of your consciousness but you have neither the will nor the ability to find the answers. Perhaps it is too early in the process for there to be any immediate answers.

You go to bed at night exhausted by worry; you sleep restlessly and wake with a dull ache that does not go away. You trudge through each fog-filled day with a heavy heart and no apparent release in sight, release from the churning thoughts that relentlessly occupy your days and the long sleepless nights. Keeping it all to yourself makes it more difficult to cope. Overcome your feelings of embarrassment and tell those close to you what is happening, although, as I mentioned in the last chapter, it is preferable to discuss all the more intricate details with a counsellor who will not take sides or judge you in any way. Whatever you feel, you haven't failed. But you do have to cope with one of the hands which life has now dealt you. Others can give you the moral support which you need and which is so important not only at this stage but at all the subsequent ones.

Your feelings should not be ignored. See your doctor if, as it often does, the shock manifests itself in physical or psychological ways. Do not be afraid to discuss what has happened and how you are feeling. The shock is real and you should try to get whatever help you need to get through this stage. It is preferable to have counselling sooner rather than later. It will help you come to terms with what has happened or is happening and assist you in making decisions.

It is at this stage that marriage or relationship counselling can be most beneficial. When emotions are so raw and feelings so close to the surface, you may both be willing to expose your innermost needs, wants and grievances. This can pave the way towards a reconciliation, if this is what you both want. Complaints can be aired and accusations made. If there is to be any hope of reconciliation, they will need to be dealt with and then put behind you to make way for a new start ahead. Swallow your pride, decide what it is that you want and do your best to summon up the energy to get it. It does take two, however, and you will both need to have the same goal and commitment to make it work.

## Children

All this time you will be in shock, one moment caring more than anything in the world, and the next not caring at all, wanting to curl up into a little ball, only resurfacing when it is all over. If the children have not yet been told, as suggested in the previous stage, they need to be informed of the situation. They will be aware of the tension and stress both parents are experiencing. At times, it may appear that the stages overlap. Although the stages are quite distinct from each other, this overlapping is not unusual during the transition from one stage to another.

> Fiona and Phil remained in the same household despite their apparent wish to divorce. They are in their mid-thirties and have two sons aged seven and five. Phil wandered around the house morose and depressed, crying constantly, telling the children that their mum wanted him to leave and he had nowhere to go. Fiona, also distressed, tried to reassure the children and not discuss the issues in front of them. But Phil always seemed to choose to have arguments and tearful confrontations precisely when the children were around. In shock and emotionally low, Phil was doing whatever he could to avoid the real issues and face up to his feelings of shock, even if it meant involving the children.

> After Graham left the home, Jane refused to allow him any contact with his two daughters. If he telephoned, they were 'out' or the answerphone was constantly on. Whatever he did, his wife did her best to obstruct his contact with the children. He provided generously for the family, but the temptation was to cut the money if Jane's attitude did not improve.

> Jane was struggling to come to terms with coping alone, always having been financially dependant on Graham. Graham was struggling to come to terms with not seeing his beloved children every day. Each was suffering in his or her own way, each hurt and reeling from the shock of what was happening.

The person who has left or has decided that the relationship is over may not find this stage too difficult. If you have a new partner, you may want to deal with the breakdown by doing nothing. You want to be free to pursue and develop your new relationship. You do not want to be burdened with wild accusations, confronted by hysterical outbursts or emotionally blackmailed by your spouse. If you have children, you will want to see them and enjoy time with them. You may want to introduce them to your new partner without feeling that you will be criticised if you do.

You may, however, feel too guilty to believe that you are entitled to anything or to do anything about it. It is very important not to feel compelled to settle anything either in relation to the children or the finances under the shroud of 'guilt'. Contrary to what you think, it is highly unlikely to bring the matter to a speedy close. That will happen only when your partner is ready to let go emotionally – whatever you offer at this stage is unlikely to be enough. At the end of the day, guilt is not a factor taken into account by the courts. The so-called guilty party is not going to be financially penalised or deprived of the children unless there are exceptional circumstances.

The children will no doubt be bewildered and scared. You probably feel bewildered and scared, too. At this time, there is so much uncertainty about the future, so much fear of the unknown, that it is preferable not to make any major decisions about anything. Time is what is needed to get through this stage and there is no short cut. You may be feeling fragile and afraid. Take one day at a time and do not allow anyone to try to pressurise you into taking any steps that you do not want to take.

Try to be particularly perceptive towards the often silent signals children give in times of uncertainty, fear and distress. Remember that each child may react in a different way at different times and will therefore need different support from you and others. Encourage the children to talk to you about their concerns. If they are unable or unwilling to talk to you, try to encourage them to talk to a close friend or other family member. Be reassuring in your answers to questions. Try not to attribute blame to the other parent even if you want to. If the children ask questions to which you do not have the answers, then tell them that.

It is important not to make promises to the children that you may not be able to keep. A common example at this stage is promising the children that they will not have to move, which may ultimately prove to be impossible. Try not to give the children conflicting messages about the future or the other parent. Try to be as consistent as possible in the circumstances and take one step at a time.

It is going to be a particularly difficult time for you, trying to remain strong and consistent for the children and yourself, yet often feeling so empty and hurt that you do not know how you will find the strength to carry on. Having children often forces you to be strong and forces you to keep going. They need you, they depend on you and they rely on you.

One of the most difficult stages is when one of you moves out of the home. Usually, but not always, it is the husband leaving the wife and the children in the matrimonial home. At other times, one parent takes the children and moves out. You may feel relieved to have the place to yourself or you may feel drained and empty at the loss you feel.

If you have the children with you, how do they feel? How do you cope with their emotions when you are struggling to cope with your own? Do they miss dad dreadfully? Do they talk about the separation or are they scared of your reaction? And how do you react if the children want to talk about the parent who has left? You may find it terribly hard to answer their questions. You may find yourself saying all the things you promised yourself you would not say to the children and yet you cannot help yourself.

Do the children play up, cry for dad or become disruptive and angry? Some children feel that they are expected to or assume the parental role and try to take care of you. Discourage this, as it is only their way of trying to deny how helpless they feel. Show them that you understand their feelings of helplessness and that you will all get through it.

And what about the dad who has left? What if you are a doting dad who was home most nights to see the children? How do you feel? From the hustle and bustle of family life, you may be confined to a miserable bedsit or accommodation that is much smaller than your home, empty, bare and unwelcoming. You are no longer able to see your children every day and that may be breaking your heart as well as theirs.

The early stages of separation are very difficult for the family. In a way, one or both of you want immediate resolutions to long-term problems. Continual financial support is required to keep two households running and uncertainty may exist as to whether or not this will be provided or even be possible. The parent who has left may want assurance that there will be ongoing and frequent contact with the children, but what is considered 'reasonable' or 'frequent'? Who will decide and how will it be decided?

In Section Two, I have set out the legal procedure. In essence, if you are able to agree issues in relation to the children, the courts and even solicitors need not become involved. However, if no agreement can be reached, the matter will be referred to the court which will make the ultimate decisions. It is preferable for all of you, if at all possible, to reach agreement or compromise and avoid the unnecessary costs, both emotional and financial, of court proceedings. During this stage it is important that a new routine be established for the children. Too much contact in the early stages can prolong the process of adjustment and cause the children confusion at a time when consistency and stability are crucial. It is important for the parent who has left the family home to understand this and view it not as obstruction of contact but rather as an attempt to give the children the space they need. In time, it is hoped that a schedule of contact suitable for all of you, which takes into account the needs and wishes of the children, may be agreed.

Try not to arrive at the family home demanding contact, if this has not been pre-arranged. It may still be your property, but respect the fact that as you no longer live there, it is inappropriate to behave as though you do. Furthermore, it can be highly provocative and likely to cause an argument which is best avoided in the presence of the children. Try not to telephone constantly with demands for daily contact; don't leave the telephone off the hook so that no contact can be made. If you don't call every day, it is unlikely that it will be construed as an indication of lack of interest unless, of course, you have promised to call. If you promise to call at a particular time, then make sure that you do so. If you think it may be difficult, then don't make such promises.

The above issues are but a few examples of what parents are tempted to do or actually do during this stage. Try to step back and see how the children feel, and think of ways in which you can help them overcome the problems which arise during the early stages of separation rather than unwittingly making it more difficult for them. Whatever you feel about each other, try to put your feelings for the children first and help ease the pressure for them. They do not need to be caught in the crossfire of emotions and will be relieved if you can protect them from it.

## Violence

You will each need time to adjust to your actions. Very hurtful words may have been hurled at each other in the heat of an argument, designed to hurt but perhaps really a transferral of guilt or of your own hurt. Either or both of you may have been reduced to violence or a repeat of previous violence. Any violence or threats of violence can give rise to criminal charges and injunctions which can result in your being excluded from your home if you still live together and even a prison sentence. Injunctions are unpleasant, serious and can be very expensive.

The best one can do, if there has been violence, is to stay away from each other or out of each other's way as much as possible until the situation starts to settle down a bit, which it will. Seek advice and guidance from your solicitor and counsellor if you have one. At all stages, your solicitor can and will act as a buffer between you and your partner.

## The options

If you have made a decision or feel fairly close to making one, there are numbers of options available, namely:

- Attend counselling either separately or together and work towards a reconciliation;
- Attend mediation to consider the separation;
- Negotiate through solicitors;
- Start divorce proceedings.

Initial discussions through solicitors can take place with regard to the arrangements for the children and the finances. If you attend couple counselling, it can help you move towards a firmer decision about what it is that you want, but whatever you do, don't let others rush you.

## Mediation

Mediation is an option that enables you to try to resolve the issues between you in a safe and impartial forum together with trained mediators. However, for mediation to prove successful, you both need to be fairly committed to reaching a resolution. It may be that mediation is not right at the present time but it may be right in a few months' time. You can go to mediation at any time and, as the process is entirely voluntary, you are not committed to any particular time scale or number of sessions. Mediation can cover all elements of the separation and divorce, including how to tell the children and what will happen on an interim basis with maintenance. Together you set the agenda and the pace.

## Taking time

Your solicitor may have told you that you need to start to gather information about the finances. If you can barely get out of bed each morning, or are unable to focus on anything of any more substance than what to wear or what to feed the family at the next meal, this is the last thing you are going to be able to do or even want to do. So, unless your solicitor is under pressure from your spouse's solicitor by virtue of court deadlines, which I explain in detail in Section Two, advise your solicitor of how you feel, and shelve this task until you feel stronger, which you will in time.

Time is what is needed to get through this stage. There is no short cut, no quick way to get through it; one day you will wake up and feel a bit stronger. The feeling of numbness will wear off and you will feel able to start picking up the pieces of your life. The children are also having to cope with changes in their lives, watching mum and dad insecure, weepy and distressed and not knowing what to do, wanting them both all the time, and they too will emerge from this stage, probably more quickly than you.

The key word for this stage is space, space for you both and for the children. Exploring each alternative, you will be able to determine for yourself the right direction to go. Give yourself the space you need and try to give your partner space as well. You are both embarking on a difficult path for which you need strength. Use this time to let what is happening sink in. Gather and build the energy you will need. It is not a time to make any other major decisions as you will find that far too overwhelming; concentrate on smaller, everyday tasks which are manageable.

Allow the children space, allow your partner space and this then will give you the space which, whether you recognise it or not, you also need. You may even feel quite relieved to have time and space within which to gather your own emotions.

Try to develop an interest or hobby, something for you, something perhaps which you always wanted to try but didn't. It will provide a new outlet where you can meet new people, people who will meet you as an individual, not as part of the couple which you once were.

## Stage 3
# Anger

The anger that erupts during this stage will strike out of the blue and can be explosive. You are unable to say your partner's name without spitting venom, referring to each other in vituperative terms. How dare someone do this to you? How dare someone treat you in this way? How dare the person you once loved, and perhaps still do, humiliate and hurt you so badly? How dare people snub or dare to judge you or your family?

All you want or think that you want is revenge and you imagine ways in which to expel the anger and get revenge to teach your partner a lesson. From being dulled by shock, you are now fired with anger. Your mind is consumed with thoughts of how to destroy the other and cause hurt greater than that which you have suffered. You want your partner to suffer, to regret what has happened, to come back crying and begging for forgiveness only so that you can reject him or her and your partner can know how it feels.

You swing from dreaming of acts of revenge to pure anger to feeling sad, pathetic and insecure. One moment the depth of anger is so great it frightens you; the next you want to run, begging forgiveness for you do not know what. During the troughs, you convince yourself that it must all be your fault, that you are entirely to blame, even though during moments of rational thought you know that is not true. You are pulled along a rollercoaster of emotions, frequently out of control.

## Counselling

If you are not already having counselling, it is during this stage that you should very seriously consider it. This stage, although it tends to be short, is also an extremely difficult one. Without warning, something or someone will trigger you and you are likely to react in an entirely unpredictable, uncharacteristic and often regrettable way. It is during these explosive episodes that you need someone for you, someone who will not judge you, criticise you or fire you up. You need a skilled professional who will guide you through the phase, for that is what it is, and over time help you to change your response so that you act in a positive way rather than react in a negative way.

Suzanna was in the midst of an acrimonious divorce, her husband crying poverty whilst taking exotic vacations with his girlfriend. When Suzanna found out that they were due to fly first class to Mexico, his third holiday in as many months, and had bought himself a little red convertible sports car, she lost control. Without consulting me, for she knew full well that I would do my utmost to dissuade her from such an action, she sent an e-mail to every single person they knew, including all his business associates. She informed them of his sexual perversions, that she thought he was a failure in bed and she set out the sorry tale of their marriage for all to read. Of course, once she pressed the 'send' key, the message went to all and sundry. The result was that her husband applied for an injunction against her.

Initially she was delighted by her actions, but as she started to calm down she realised what she had done. Her deed was irreversible. There was nothing she could do about it, and in time she deeply regretted her actions. What had she hoped to achieve – revenge, sympathy? Did she achieve it and, if so, at what cost? It certainly did not reflect well on her. After that incident, she took my advice to seek counselling. The next time there was an incident which triggered her temper, and there would be a next time, she could pick up the telephone and call her counsellor. She could see her counsellor when she was in crisis and learn how to channel her anger in a way less damaging to her in the long run.

## Aggressive behaviour

Anger often precedes the process of letting go. You should try to acknowledge the real reason for your anger, which can pave the way towards understanding and acceptance of the situation. The temptation to use the children or money as an excuse for further anger and revenge is ever-present. This should, however, be avoided at all costs. The children are innocent victims and should not be drawn into the arena, however ferocious the battle.

Inevitably, solicitors will by now be involved and letters will be passing between them. Financial disclosure will have to take place and this requires disclosure of everything and anything financial, be it yours, your partner's or something owned jointly. It all falls into the pot to be divided, irrespective of who earned it or inherited it and irrespective of the reason for the breakdown of the marriage. Everything, in theory, is up for grabs! Avoid the temptation of preventing the children seeing the other parent or of stopping paying money as a way of punishing your partner. Unfortunately, all this will do is exacerbate the situation, and the longer it continues, the more acrimonious the separation becomes.

Aggressive and spiteful letters may come from your partner. The aim of these letters, and often telephone calls too, may well be to provoke you until you lose control. You may receive letters from your partner's solicitor which anger you. They may detail your partner's perspective of incidents, which is completely different from yours. They may contain inflammatory allegations against you. These letters will need to be answered, but not in a similarly aggressive way. Being drawn into correspondence like this is not only likely to add fuel to the fire, but may make the prospects of any agreement, let alone an amicable one, highly unlikely and delay realistic negotiations.

At this stage it is often easy to be side-tracked by the smaller issues such as the most recent disagreement. You lose track of what it is that you are trying to achieve in the long term: a divorce, amicable if possible, with suitable arrangements for the children and a fair financial settlement. Of course this may not be what you feel at this stage, but as you move through the various stages, you will realise that there is little point in seeking the impossible, destroying whatever and whomever crosses your path. Your solicitor and counsellor are the people who can help you remain focused on your long-term goals whilst helping you cope with the short-term issues that are at times so overwhelming and difficult that you lose perspective.

Remember that this is only a phase and will pass, and whilst in it, acknowledge it and deal with it. Act positively rather than reacting negatively. You will never change your partner and if your partner was unpleasant when you were married, you cannot seriously expect that person to become more pleasant during the divorce. He or she will become worse and all the traits that you despised or which upset you when you were together will become more extreme. With the benefit of counselling, you can learn to change your response to your partner's behaviour so that what used to enrage you no longer does.

However strong the temptation, it important during this stage that you do not act on your anger. But if you do, don't be too hard on yourself, for it is an incredibly difficult time and at times you will feel like exploding with anger. Try to learn from your reactions; identify what triggered your response and aim to rise above it next time.

In many cases, the behaviour between couples after separation and during divorce is a replay of behaviour during the marriage. Your partner knows precisely how to wind you up and upset you. For as long as you continue to react as you did during your relationship, the cycle of destructive behaviour is likely to continue. It is up to you to change the pattern, for changing your soon-to-be-ex is impossible.

## Revenge

It is during this stage that people behave in the most outrageous and dramatic ways.

> In a fit of anger, after yet another row about the time Tim spent at the pub, Jane cut the sleeves off all of Tim's suits and then threw them and his other belongings out of the bedroom window, leaving them strewn across the garden in the pouring rain.

> When Martha called her husband to tell him that the car wouldn't start and asked for the RAC registration details, he was dismissive and uninterested. She had to get to school to collect the children and then take them to the dentist and he didn't offer to collect the children or to help in any way. He just didn't seem to be bothered at all. She put down the telephone, went to his prized and valued record collection and systematically snapped each one in half. She then felt so drained that she wept and wept and wept.

> Ryan emptied out on to the floor the contents of all the boxes he could find in the kitchen after Judy refused to cook him dinner. He wanted to continue to play

happy families, not listening and not hearing when Judy told him the marriage was over. He then broke the chairs so no one could sit at the table and eat dinner.

You both need time to recover and you need to ensure that you avoid confrontational situations. If during this stage you find yourself about to do something which you know will be in anger and which you will regret, find ways to regain control of yourself: take a walk; go outside and kick a tree; cook; play squash; exercise. But whatever you do, try your best not to do anything that can be physically dangerous, emotionally damaging or cause legal action to be taken against you. And, of course, if you are in counselling, you will have your counsellor to turn to at moments of crisis.

## Coping with the anger

When a confrontational situation arises, if you are able to be rational, try asking yourself:

- What is it that I am trying to achieve?
- Will it affect my child?

When John arrived to collect his four-year-old daughter for contact and refused to put her in her car seat, whom was he really trying to punish?

What did Mark achieve by refusing to disclose his company accounts? He increased the legal costs substantially and added to his legal bill.

May refused to allow Jack under any circumstances to see the children if he was with his new girlfriend. She was effectively blocking contact when the children needed to see their dad. And, in a state of desperation, she destroyed his precious bonsai trees whilst the children stood by watching. She felt on the edge, and was having difficulty controlling her anger. These actions were not only out of character but also out of control.

## Reconciliation

Try to recognise the feelings of anger as they erupt and have a plan of action for dealing with these them when they arise. Try not to leave yourself feeling emotionally stranded to the point of losing control. Despite all that has happened, in your heart you may still want to be together, you may want to try again and don't know how. It is really not too late, provided you both want the same thing.

At this stage, it can be difficult to know how to express your feelings or how best to make the right approach. The messages which your outraged behaviour is sending may be entirely the opposite of what you really want. Discuss this with your solicitor or counsellor. Your solicitor can make sure that, wherever possible, no further legal steps are taken whilst you are undecided. You are the driver: in your case you decide what to do, and if you want to reconcile, you will be encouraged to do so.

You need to be as sure as possible that a divorce is right. It is not a time to be proud; you need to say what you feel before it is too late. Never feel embarrassed about your indecision or obliged to apologise to anyone. If you both want to reconcile, then do so – you can at any time until decree absolute. I have had many clients who have successfully reconciled and so halted legal proceedings.

## Children

If you are the parent who has left, you may desperately want to see the children every day. Initially, hard as it may be, try not to demand more than you know your partner will permit, as all you will do is stir up enormous conflict, frequently in the presence of the children and with little satisfaction. This does not mean that in time you will not get more contact. It is likely to pave the way for more contact when the situation has calmed down a little, particularly if you are able to give each other some space.

Very often the parent who is left with the children feels particularly vulnerable. Demanding too much contact too soon after separation can add to those feelings. Your partner may feel that you are being threatening and controlling, and fear that increased contact will result in your luring the children away. Rather than becoming more and more demanding, the better way is to reassure your partner that you are not trying to take the children away. If your partner does not feel threatened, you are likely to find that contact is increased. It is also important to consider what is truly best for the children during these early stages, however hard that may be.

Contact, which means the frequency of visits, and residence of the children (with whom the children live on a day-to-day basis) are always subject to review and variation if the circumstances warrant it. By stepping back a little, you are in a way removing the power that your former partner can exert over you. But, more importantly, you are ensuring, that the children are not being drawn into the battlefield because of your behaviour.

You may find that each time you go to collect the children, your partner attempts to provoke an argument. Before you know it, you are screaming at each other. Do your best to avoid these confrontations and, whatever you do, do not become threatening or violent. You will, at worst, be leaving yourself open to an injunction being taken out against you; at best, there will be a blow-by-blow account of the incident recorded in a letter from your former partner's solicitor. Learn to walk away: it is more effective and enables you to retain your dignity.

If you are the one who has been left with the children, try not to let your anger with your former partner spill over into contact with the children. This is easier said than done, but however hard it is, it is likely to help your children during the traumatic time that follows separation. For the sake of your children, do your utmost to promote a good ongoing relationship with their other parent. No doubt you are angry with each other, and probably for good reason, but try not to allow your anger with each other to interfere with the relationship that you each have with the children. Your children need both parents and neither of you can be replaced.

The cause of the separation will often set the tone, at least initially, for the way in which contact takes place. If the separation is against your wishes, or you feel that you were the one forced out, the anger which you experience can be quite vicious. Anger can lead to hate, which can lead to a wish for revenge, and to what end? If you are angry, acknowledge your anger, accept it and deal with it. This may sound simplistic, but there really is no option. Try not to take it out directly or indirectly on the children.

If dad wants to telephone the children, let him. It may happen that when he calls them, they do not want to talk to him. Try not to view this as a victory – it is really not one. Ask yourself why the children feel that way. They may feel uncomfortable about talking to him if you are in the room. Perhaps you are not even giving them the chance to talk to him, and are simply leaving the answerphone on. Dad calls and leaves a message and all the while the children are in the next room and can hear the message which he leaves. Who is punishing whom?

Unless there are grounds for serious concern, such as violence, sexual abuse or some other real danger to them, children need to be able to move freely between both parents. They should be allowed to speak freely to each parent and feel confident that, in so doing, they are not betraying either parent. They can only do this with your support – how you really feel is irrelevant.

During the angry stage, you may well find yourself behaving or reacting in any of the ways detailed below. Rather than being consumed with guilt about what you may be doing to the children by your inability to respond appropriately, and rather than being gleeful at just how angry your behaviour is making your partner, try to think how the children are feeling. You may well be angry and do some really awful things; but can you see how the children feel? In the examples that follow, bear that thought in mind so that you can develop the ability to protect the children.

You may not always be able to control your anger, and perhaps in trying to do so you are setting yourself an unrealistic goal. But if you are aware of what is happening and you understand why, you will be able to look, reflect and act rather than react thoughtlessly. Throughout the process your partner may continue to provoke and harass you to the extent that self-control is impossible. Just do your best.

So if, for example, dad is the one who leaves (and the reverse could be the same if mum is the one to leave), consider the following carefully.

## Children and telephone calls

If dad wants to telephone every day to talk to the children, can you let him? You may find it painful, but then so may the children find it painful not speaking to their dad. At the time of separation more than ever, they need to know that, despite his leaving, he still loves them. If calls are blocked, they may feel that they are to blame or, even worse, that he really does not care about them after all.

The most common excuses given for not allowing regular telephone calls are that the children are busy, out, in the bath, watching TV, doing homework, eating, playing or do not want to talk. At times these reasons may be genuine; you must accept and understand them. Allow the other parent to call later at a more convenient time. Sometimes the children become upset after a call and you wish to protect them and avoid upset.

If the children do speak to their dad on the telephone, try to leave them alone, do not hover around them in an attempt to listen in on the call, and do not interrupt the calls with demands for money or call him a lying cheating good-for-nothing. Similarly, if you are the caller, it does not help to criticise the other parent, ask questions about finances or social life or tell the children how desperately unhappy you are and that it's all that 'wicked woman's/man's' fault.

Try to consider how the children feel. Whatever either of you says or does, you are still the children's parents. Your partner may well be all the things you call him or her, and more, and you may have every reason for feeling the way that you do. But try not to involve the children. Try to contain the anger that you feel between the two of you. The children are and must remain a separate issue.

## Contact visits

The frequency of contact visits really does depend on you both. I have clients who have managed successfully to have an arrangement of joint or co-parenting and others who argue each and every weekend. As a rule of thumb, and all things being equal, if you can't agree on contact between you, alternating weekends and sharing school holidays is considered to be reasonable. But this should not in any way be seen as ideal. The ideal situation is when parents can settle down into a flexible routine of contact and continue to co-parent as much as possible. This, however, may not be possible in the early stages of breakdown and separation, as emotions are too ragged and close to the surface to allow one or both of you to be rational or reasonable.

So what are the most common problems which arise time and again over contact? Firstly, setting up and arranging contact itself. Questions which may be asked are:

- Where are you going to take the children?
- What time will they be collected and returned?

- Can they sleep over?
- How often will contact take place?
- What about the new partner?
- What about grandparents and cousins?

During the initial stages of separation, the parent who has left may want to see the children every day and the other parent may want to limit contact. Looking at it from the perspective of the parent with care, that parent will need to establish a new routine with the children and they will have to go through a period of adjustment.

The parent with care may also enjoy being the one to decide when the children will see their other parent. Try to consider why you feel this way and try not to use the children in order to punish your partner for something which had nothing to do with the children.

Think very carefully about the motivation behind your actions – whom are you really trying to punish? By punishing your former partner, you may also be punishing your children. Is that what you really want? These situations have strange ways of backfiring, sometimes at the cost of the children. Scrutinise your motives and think of the effect that your actions may have on the children.

Below are examples of unreasonable or thoughtless behaviour – see if you recognise any. Although, in most cases, it is the mother who is the parent with care, the trend is changing and it is becoming less unusual for fathers to be the main carer of children. All the examples below are equally applicable to mothers and fathers.

- Arranging contact to take place but when dad/mum arrives, everyone has gone out.

- Messing dad/mum around, making them wait, wasting their day, giving some excuse to the children and most of all making him/her suffer.

- When dad/mum arrives to collect the children, opening the front door with the safety chain intact, the children hovering in the background, and demanding more money otherwise 'you can't take them!' Have you ever thought about how that makes the children feel? They love their dad/mum and miss the other parent, yet money is being demanded for them. They will be thinking that they would rather do without the things mum/dad says that they need just to avoid the fights and to be able to see the other parent. Perhaps they should eat less and then more money for food would not be necessary! Children tend to become very self-conscious and may be inclined mistakenly to blame themselves.

- When dad/mum arrives to collect the children, opening the door, shoving them out and slamming the door in his/her face.

- Making dad/mum wait in the car because the tension between you is so bad that you can't be anywhere near each other. Making him/her wait as long as possible before you let the children go out. (The children of course know the other parent is out there and waiting because they can see out of the window.)

- Not being at home when the children are returned home so that they have to wait – again.

- Priming the children to find out whatever they can about the other parent's new lifestyle and then interrogating them as soon as they get home. Also making them promise not to tell the other parent about anything which they do, or whom you see. This can create feelings of guilt and confusion for the children.

What about the cases where dad/mum arrives to collect the children, is aggressive and abusive towards the other parent in their presence and then wonders why the children start crying and do not want to go with him/her? Or when dad/mum arrives drunk or refuses to put the children in car seats just to wind the other parent up? The safety of the children is paramount. Don't play games with the lives of your children.

When the children are upset and distraught, they are often asked to decide if they want to go with the other parent or not. Why should children be placed in such an untenable position, having to choose? Your partner may well be behaving in an appalling way in relation to the finances, and you are quite justified in being furious. There you are, left with the children, insufficient or no money, whilst he drives around in a fancy new sports car, apparently living it up, or she is dripping is expensive jewellery from her new man. For you there is no money, but when he/she takes the children out, they spend a fortune on expensive outings and toys when you would prefer the money for basics. If you need more money, do something about it, but not by using the children. Speak to your solicitor, who will advise and assist you where possible.

These are games you may both play – you are making contact difficult because you are not paid enough money or is it that you are not paid enough money because you make contact difficult? And who suffers? I believe everyone suffers, and if nothing else is possible, at least try aim towards limiting the suffering of your children, for they do suffer when caught between you in your conflict.

These examples are not meant to make you feel guilty but rather to identify the problems. Firstly you need to be aware that you are not the only one who reacts in the ways in which you do – these situations inevitably occur in one form or another within every family. Secondly, and more importantly, if you are able to recognise what is happening, you will be able to avoid or limit the occurrence of such a situation.

All of these situations occur because of the acute distress experienced by you, the parent. You should try to look at yourself and the children and honestly ask yourself: what is it that I am trying to prove and what is the effect on my child?

This is a period of adjustment for all of you. You will need time to adjust to the change and find, though trial and error, what contact is best. Sometimes all the children will go out, and sometimes one will have a party to go to or some other activity. Don't take it personally that your child does not want to come with you or wants to go to a party, that he or she does not want to see you. By the same token, don't gloat if you think your child doesn't want to see the other parent – it is not a victory.

## Divorce proceedings

On the divorce front, you may at this stage find yourself trying to block the divorce. There is little point in defending a divorce because inevitably the divorce will be granted. Hard as it may seem, the actual divorce is the easiest issue to resolve, whilst the issues arising from problems over the children and division of the finances are more complicated. Generally the actual grounds for the divorce itself have no bearing on either the division of the finances or rights over the children. So, for example, the person who has committed adultery and is divorced for that reason is not penalised in the financial settlement. The Divorce Law Reform which comes into effect at the end of the 1990s, does away with 'fault' (see page 0) completely.

This is a particularly difficult stage but, thankfully, a fairly short-lived one. It affects both you and the children. It is not the stage for contemplating seriously any basis for a settlement. It is rather a time to concentrate on getting the ground work out of the way, setting the scene for negotiations to take place in due course.

There are four main issues or aspects which will need to be resolved and which are detailed in Section Two. These are:

1. The separation or the divorce itself;
2. What will happen to the children;
3. How the assets will be divided;
4. What maintenance will be payable.

All of these issues will have to be dealt with, although not necessarily at the same time. In fact, it is seldom that all issues are agreed simultaneously, particularly as everyone needs time to adjust emotionally to the breakdown and to leading lives apart from each other. And until both of you are emotionally ready to let go and move on, much as you may say that you want to, you will not be able to reach agreement. I have found that whatever is suggested as a way of settling the matter at this stage invariably fails or is unrealistic. Neither of you is in a suitable emotional state for finalising things. The time should be used for preparation rather than final negotiation.

## Mediation

Mediation is an option that should be considered and at this stage it can help enormously in finding workable solutions to problems over contact. Mediation enables both of you to consider what is in dispute, to weigh up the options and then try to find a solution. Mediation is not about getting you back together but about assisting you in an amicable separation and divorce and I explain it in more detail in Section Two. Mediation is not suitable for everyone, and for it to be successful you must both have a genuine wish to redress the conflict and reach a workable agreement. It will not work if one of you attends with the intention of delaying matters, giving others the impression that you are co-operating whereas it is really a ploy to manipulate or delay. It may be that during the angry stage mediation is not appropriate but could be later on.

It is sometimes only in a forum such as the one which mediation provides that you are both able to vent your feelings, your anger, disappointments and fears. You are both present but with independent impartial professionals who can keep the session focused.

Problems involving contact with the children should not be left unresolved. If contact is being denied, discuss with your solicitor the steps that can be taken. These are set out in Section Two. If contact proves difficult or is denied altogether, an application can be made to court for contact to be defined. Court proceedings, however, should only be used as a last resort.

Being aware of what you are doing, identifying this stage and recognising the problems attributable to your anger can help you try to channel your energies in a positive and constructive way rather than reacting wildly and in a manner which you may regret later.

## Stage 4
# Pain

By now, you probably know whether there is a chance of reconciliation or if a divorce is inevitable. Remember that, at any time, if you both want to reconcile, you can and should do so. If you have started divorce proceedings, you will find the process painstakingly slow, with few visible results. A divorce, which includes sorting out any problems about the children and the finances, can take anything from six to nine months (this is exceptional) to the more usual period of two to three years. It is not usually in your interest to try to speed up the legal process because until you are both emotionally ready to let go, you won't settle the issues.

Solicitors are corresponding with each other about your life and your future, and you probably feel in a state of flux. Your anger will have abated, although it still erupts from time to time. Your confidence will have hit an all-time low, and with very little self-esteem, you may be afraid that you will never pick up the pieces of your life.

Depending where you are in dealing with the finances, disclosure may be coming in dribs and drabs and if your partner is not pushing for information, or has not given any either, there is no need to rush. Your solicitor or your partner's solicitor may be pestering you with letters, requesting or demanding information. You have neither the energy nor the inclination even to read the letters, let alone reply to them. The temptation is to bin them – you wish everyone would leave you alone. If, however, you want it all sorted out sooner rather than later, it may be that proceedings are already under way, in which case you will both be bound to the timetable imposed by the proceedings and explained in greater detail in Section Two. Frustration with the whole process is often reflected in reluctance to co-operate, be it in relation to contact with the children, financial disclosure or maintenance.

What takes the place of anger is pain – deep, intense pain which just does not go away. If you have separated, you may have started to adjust to life without the other. The pain will be there, but will gradually decrease in intensity and frequency. You will find that, whereas previously your thoughts were constantly on your partner and the breakdown, short periods of time will pass when you have concentrated on the task before you, and, to your surprise, have not thought about your partner.

## Moving out

If you want your partner to leave, but your partner refuses to do so until the divorce or the finances are sorted out, the tension in the household may feel suffocating and unbearable. It is not always possible to force a partner to leave the joint home and it is always preferable if one of you leaves of your own accord and by agreement. Your partner may resist the move for any number of reasons, the usual one being to punish you, to force a financial settlement or because your partner does not accept that the relationship is over and hopes that, given time, you will change your mind. If there is nowhere else to go, lack of money may make a move impossible until the finances are sorted out and the property is sold.

You live in limbo, suffering from having to see each other every day, and although emotionally you have separated, physically you have not: your home no longer provides the privacy or solitude you so desire. You have to share your space with someone who has become a stranger. It may reach the point where your partner comes and goes as an intrusive lodger. If you do have a room to call your own during this stage, you may have to lock it, as you know that, in your absence, your partner searches through your personal belongings looking for information that may not even exist. Your partner may continue to be as obnoxious as possible, constantly wearing you down, sometimes returning home at night and sometimes not.

> **Sheila and Adam continued to live in the same household during the divorce. Adam did move out for a few days, only to return with his father who informed Sheila that he had come to stay until the divorce was over. Sheila became hysterical as now not only was Adam making her life unbearable, but she also**

had her father-in-law following her around, interfering and critical. She was on the verge of a nervous breakdown, locking herself in the bathroom, crying uncontrollably. She had turned her bedroom into a bedsit where she and the children effectively lived when Adam and his father were in the house. In this case, it was necessary to seek assistance from the court to have both Adam and his father removed from the property, as the situation had become intolerable for Sheila. It took a long time for Sheila to recover from the trauma and Adam's threatening and unreasonable attitude impacted on his relationship with his children. They had witnessed far too much for them to simply forget and to this day remain wary of Adam.

Barry arrived at my office ashen, clutching a sheaf of papers in his hands. His wife, Holly, had made an application to court for an order that he be removed permanently from the property alleging, falsely he claimed, that he had physically and mentally abused her. He told me that there was no truth in any of the allegations, all of which had been manufactured in an attempt to get him to leave the home. Barry wanted to fight the case in court and return home. I have no doubt that he would have succeeded if he had fought the case, and in all likelihood his wife would have been ordered to pay his legal costs. But at what personal cost? It was quite apparent that if Barry did return home, Holly would try again to get him out, provoking or fabricating arguments, and all the while the children would be exposed to the non-stop battles.

The more sensible way of dealing with the matter would be for Barry to leave the property voluntarily, making it clear that there was no truth in his wife's allegations. Initially he was reluctant to follow this route, feeling that by doing so Holly would have 'won'. Yes, she had succeeded in getting him to leave, but in truth, although there had been no emotional or physical abuse as alleged, the tension at home had become unbearable, even for him. He knew that it would be much better for the children if they were exposed to less tension, but quite understandably, he found it very difficult to leave his home, his children and his security. In doing so, he had to face the reality that the separation was to be permanent and he was not ready to do this.

## Delaying tactics

At times, you want everything to happen much faster than it does and you want it all to be over. Yet it drags on and on, solicitors' letters going backwards and forwards, always asking for more information, the senders apparently never satisfied with the information that has been provided. Your partner may show all the right signs of being ready, willing and able to negotiate and move towards a settlement, whereas in reality he or she is merely playing mind games and using delaying tactics. You may feel at the end of your tether and unable to take the strain much longer.

> Vicky and Leonard appeared to be close to reaching an agreement – all that was standing in the way was the chess set. Leonard knew that Vicky had it, but she insisted that she did not. It was of sentimental value to Leonard and he was determined that it be returned to him. On the face of it, it seemed that the whole deal was dependent upon the chess set, but the real issue was Vicky not being ready to let go. She did not play chess and had no use for the chess set. She was holding on to to it because she knew that until Leonard got it back, the divorce would not be finalised. Eventually she did return it to him – much later on in the process – and the black castle was missing! The pieces were hand-carved and irreplaceable.

> Martin and Carol thought that they were close to reaching an agreement, but for the video camera and piano which each wanted. Neither was prepared to let the other have them and they were at a stalemate. The whole settlement looked doomed to failure because of those two items. They were about to compromise, with Martin keeping the piano, when he unexpectedly decided that he wanted the grandfather clock that was a family heirloom of Carol's. Carol was now so exhausted by the whole process that she just wanted let him have the lot – she no longer had the energy to argue.

> Carol needed to be coaxed to stick to her guns. Whatever she had offered Martin at this point would not have been enough. Martin was not ready to let go, so he kept moving the goal posts. Fortunately, he would get over this stage, and an agreement, a fair one, was reached.

## Children

If you are being denied proper or regular contact with your children, you will be missing them terribly. Try your utmost not to involve the children in disputes with your partner and don't let them feel that they have contributed to the breakdown – such guilt can be emotionally damaging in both the short and long term. Never forget that the children also suffer. They have to come to terms with their parents' divorce, and, sooner or later, with living with only one parent. Inevitably the children feel that they are in some way to blame. Some believe that they can get their parents to love each other again. Some try to intercept the crossfire of their two warring parents.

A difficult concept for children to grasp is that they can continue to love both parents despite the fact that their parents no longer love each other. They must be encouraged to retain their feelings for both parents and the parents must not constantly refer to each other in derogatory terms, pointing out the faults of the other and expecting the children to take sides. Even though you are in pain, try to ease the pain of your children. They need to know that both parents love them and neither parent blames them. Try not to place the burden of separation, even unconsciously, on the children. If you feel that this is happening, seek help. Mediation can sometimes provide the forum for parents to discuss the problems that arise in relation to the children. With both parents together, and with the help of trained mediators, you may find that you are able to approach the issues in a way with which you both feel comfortable and which will be in the interests of the children. When there are particular problems concerning older children, the mediators can see the children, not allowing the children to make decisions but rather letting them be heard.

Conflict over the children may by now have started to die down, although if your partner is stuck in the stage of anger, the problems will continue. Frequently, the father is placed in a 'no win' situation – if he telephones too often, he will be accused of harassment; if he calls less often, he will be accused of lack of interest. Obviously, genuinely threatening and harassing telephone calls should be avoided – if not, you could find yourself at the receiving end of an injunction, which will limit the telephone calls and perhaps even contact.

If telephone calls create problems, pre-arrange the times of calls. The children will then feel secure in the knowledge that dad loves them and is interested in them and will know when to expect your call. Dad can be up-to-date with whatever they do and continue to be actively involved in their interests. Of course, if you say that you are going to call on a particular day at a particular time, then you must make sure that you do.

If you experience continual difficulties over contact with the children, keep a diary of all telephone calls and contact. This should include attempts to speak to the children when they are 'unavailable', attempts to speak to them when the answerphone is on in a blatant move to block calls, and details of when contact takes place, should have taken place and did not take place. Use the diary to record whatever happens. In this way, if the matter goes to court, all the facts are at your fingertips and will make it much easier to argue your case before the court.

Another big area of conflict can revolve around meeting the 'other' person, the new partner. How do you both feel about this potentially explosive situation? If you refuse to allow the children to meet the new partner under any circumstances, try to ascertain the real reason for this. Do you know or hope that it will cause conflict in the new relationship?

Perhaps you fear that the children will like the new person and they will try to replace you? And what if they do like each other? Of course it will hurt, and very deeply. But is it not preferable that if there is someone else, it is someone who is kind and caring to the children? You may find that person more responsible than your partner, so you will know with certainty that when the children are with them, they will be properly cared for. In the long term, this can prove to be very positive for the children. However, it is one of the more difficult elements to accept, particularly in the early stages of separation, if you believe that the person is the cause of the breakdown.

When Christopher left the matrimonial home, he swore that he would never go back to the house or speak to Jennifer. The reason for this was that she denigrated him to such an extent that he completely lost confidence in himself. She knew how to press all the buttons that made him lose his temper and get out of control. In fact, his violent temper had been a problem in the marriage and was a cause for concern when he had contact.

Difficult as it was for Jennifer to accept, and it was very difficult for her, Christopher's girlfriend Liz was a kind, gentle woman who managed to keep Christopher calm; she knew the children were quite safe if Liz was around. Because Christopher would not talk to Jennifer on the telephone, Liz made the arrangements for contact, collected the children and in time proved to be a supportive ally and someone whom the children trusted and turned to if they were with their dad and a problem arose. Unusual situation, yes, but this illustrates how different each family is and how each family finds a solution that works for them. There are no hard-and-fast rules.

Wherever possible, any new person should be introduced to the children with careful planning and sensitivity. It is going to be difficult for the children to accept anyone new, particularly if that person is depicted as evil and wicked. Rest assured: no one can ever replace you.

Rupert is a devoted father who cherished his children above all else. When he left the matrimonial home, Alicia went out of her way to sabotage all his attempts at retaining contact with the children. When he telephoned, the answerphone was on. She then changed the telephone number without telling him. She would be out when he went to collect the children, or she would not allow them to go with him when he arrived to collect them; and when Rupert finally formed another relationship, she refused point blank to allow the children to meet his girlfriend. Rupert saw his children whenever he was allowed, under any circumstances. He knew that if he introduced the children to his girlfriend without Alicia's consent, she would stop contact altogether. So when he saw the children, he was not able to take them to his home, have them overnight or take them on holidays. But Rupert saw the children under such unreasonable conditions because he knew that if he did not agree, he would not see them at all or would have to take the matter to court, an experience to which he did not want to expose his children.

The children were denied the opportunity of becoming integrated in their dad's new life, being allocated only small windows of time in his life by their mother: unsatisfactory for all of them. But Rupert hung on and eventually Alicia passed through this stage and the pain of acknowledging that there was a new woman in Rupert's life started to ease. When I last spoke to him, all was well and the children were spending alternate weekends with him and his new partner. He could just have easily been overwhelmed by frustration and given up trying to retain contact with his children. But is that what Alicia really wanted, for the children to lose contact with their dad? I think not.

And how did Alicia justify her behaviour? Well, who knows? To others she would say it was the choice of the children. But in such situations children do not have free choice. If they say otherwise, they have to live with the wrath of their mother. Alicia could not see the effect which her reaction had on the children, on Rupert, and on contact. She, like so many others, was unable or unwilling to see beyond her pain and through the hatred which followed, unable to understand that, in punishing and hurting Rupert, In fact she was also punishing and hurting the children. The strange thing about her actions was that she was no longer alone as she too had found a new partner, but this did nothing to dilute her pain or anger against Rupert.

Many men would have lost patience, become fed up with the manipulation and stopped the constant struggle to see their children. And sadly in this case, as in so many other similar cases, the children were too young to stand on their own or say what it was they wanted. Or perhaps, having been told it so often, they actually believed what their mother told them over and over and over again. Did she really want him to stop seeing the children altogether? I would hope not, but there are cases where that appears to be precisely what the parent with care wants, and only time will reveal the long-term effects on the children, growing up without the other parent while knowing that he or she desperately wants to see them but can't.

In this type of situation, hard as it may be, try not to let your own feelings towards your partner affect contact. Continued contact is so important for your children. Try to ensure that your children are able to spend quality time with the other parent even if it does mean that they also spend time with the new partner. This may be painful and difficult for you, it may be something which you never get used to, but which will be in the children's best interests.

## Family and friends

If you find it difficult to cope with being alone and experience an overwhelming emptiness when they are all out together as a new family unit, it can be helpful for you to have company or be with friends during these times. Hard as it may be to believe, in time you will look forward to having the house to yourself. It will be a time for you, when you can be totally self-indulgent and do whatever you want, with no one needing your help, interrupting you or making demands of any sort on you.

With the best intentions in the world, family and friends will give you advice, telling you what you should do, and how you should do it. You may find the advice conflicting and contrary to what your solicitor had advised, and having to listen to all their opinions can be very confusing and stressful for you. You may still love your partner, but family and friends continue to run him or her down. You are encouraged to 'take him to the cleaners' or to 'stop paying her any money'. You know if you listen to them, it is likely to aggravate the position; if you don't, they criticise you for lack of strength. Do what feels and is right for you and try not to be adversely influenced by those around you. You will not get Brownie points for pleasing those around you, so do what it is that will lead you to acceptance and happiness.

## Counselling

Feelings of extreme pain often pass in a couple of months. If you find that somehow you seem stuck emotionally and just cannot seem to pull yourself out of this stage, I strongly recommend that you seek counselling. It is important to deal with this stage and not become cynical and bitter about the rest of your life. Moving on enables you to recover.

## Stage 5
# Hatred

While the worst stage is that of hatred, I believe it is also the turning point. Get through this stage and you are on the way towards the final stage of divorce. Generally it is an accumulation of events and the apparent lack of progress that makes you feel rage and frustration. You would gladly give up everything and start life afresh with a new name and a new identity in a new country. Your thoughts are filled with ways in which to punish your soon-to-be-ex-partner. You look back and married togetherness seems a lifetime away. You have forgotten what it is like not to struggle, emotionally and financially. Even if it were your choice, you hate your partner for making you struggle, for making you suffer, for forcing a change of lifestyle, for disrupting the children, and for not letting it all end.

Although you may be enjoying the freedom, meeting new friends and pursuing new hobbies, you still feel that you cannot get on with your life until the past has been resolved. You will feel frustrated by your contrasting emotions: on the one hand you want to move on, on the other you are still tied to the past – you can't simply delete years of memories. At times the hate is so great that you really do want to see your partner down and out in the gutter; you want your partner's life to be ruined as you believe your life has been, as a direct result of the other's behaviour.

Although the end may be in sight, one or both of you may not yet be ready for the finality of divorce. And this is the crux of the process: the combination of hate, fear and sense of loss means that each time you get close to a settlement, one or both of you sabotages the settlement, moves the goal posts and an agreement remains unattainable.

It would be foolhardy at this stage to withdraw reasonable proposals which have been put forward or to demand that unrealistic deadlines be imposed for acceptance of proposals. Probably ninety to ninety-five per cent of cases are eventually resolved by means of an agreement and in the remaining cases the court will impose an order which is generally not ideal for either side. It is costly both emotionally and financially when an agreement cannot be reached, and the outcome is determined by the court.

In this stage of hatred, Alan called, demanding that a letter be sent immediately to his wife's solicitor informing her that his offer was being increased and that if she did not accept it within forty-eight hours, all offers were to be withdrawn and he would see her in court.

Dennis sent a raging letter demanding that a final deadline be imposed on the last offer, otherwise he would walk away from his manufacturing business and they would all go belly up!

Robert stormed into the office, insistent that he would quit his job and leave the country if everything was not settled by the end of the week. It was Thursday!

Maggie viciously threatened to blackmail Leonard by exposing him to the Inland Revenue if he did not agree to give her all the assets which they had acquired during the marriage and owned jointly. They were both directors and equal shareholders in their company and her demands and threats were made despite the fact that if she carried them out, they were both implicated and she had as much to lose as him.

Glenda, aware that it was in both their interests for Harry to continue working until he turned sixty-five in order to gain the maximum benefit from his company pension, went on a campaign to have him dismissed and publicly embarrass him in order to get what she wanted from him. He had only eighteen months until retirement, yet she sent a barrage of abusive and embarrassing letters to the managing director and other members of staff as well as bombarding them with incessant telephone calls designed to humiliate Harry. Theirs was a long marriage and it was in as much her interest as Harry's for him to continue to work until he reached sixty-five. The financial rewards would be substantial if Harry worked for the next eighteen months, but Glenda, in her rage, just didn't seem to care.

Susan arrived at her meeting with me to discuss the proposal which had been put forward by her husband's solicitor on his behalf in relation to maintenance, only to tell me, yet again, that she would not allow her husband to see the children because it did not suit her, fiercely determined to fight on! She was punishing him, acting in a cold and calculated way which she knew hurt him, and placing him in a position in which he had no option but to make an application to court for proper contact with his children to be ordered.

Maria telephoned, screaming down the telephone to inform her husband that if he did not agree to what she wanted, she would sell all his antiques at the car boot sale on Saturday!

All of the above were in a fairly hysterical state, demanding the unrealistic. And all of them were frustrated by the process, on the path to self-destruction unless something could be done to halt them. But you and your partner cannot be forced to agree to a settlement until you are both ready to compromise. Before you are in a position to conclude the legal aspects of the divorce, you need to come to terms with the emotional aspects. It is only then that it will all slot into place. What was previously unattainable becomes attainable; what was previously impossible to compromise is compromised.

During this stage, you will wish that you could just run away, to escape the uncertainty and the haggling. But you cannot run away. Try to redirect your energy from hatred to developing new interests, for example, or giving your work the commitment it requires. Concentrate on building a new family unit which doesn't include your partner. The end is in sight even if it looks like it will be a bitter struggle.

# Counselling

Contact should never be a trade-off for money but only too often it is – money *versus* the children! Now you have them, now you don't! Pay me more, do as I say, go where I want and you can have them; if not, you lose! There are so many elements to this issue, elements that need to be expressed and dealt with lest you become stuck in this stage. Counselling really is the only way through.

Frank was particularly resistant to counselling, his view being 'real blokes don't do counselling'. He had become seriously depressed, his relationship with his children had deteriorated badly and so had his performance at work. He failed to achieve an important promotion, and he was convinced that it was all his wife's fault as she unreasonably refused to accept his offers of settlement. He had become obsessed with the forthcoming trial, focusing entirely on that and not beyond. Because of his inability to acknowledge the role that he played in the breakdown of the marriage, he was stuck in the hatred stage and was unable to move on. He spoke briefly to a counsellor to whom he said I could talk. The counsellor, who is very experienced and for whom I have great respect, told me of his concern about Frank. With the benefit of counselling Frank might come to terms with the breakdown and separation, which he had never wanted and which had brought to the fore unresolved issues from his past which would not simply go away. Frank was in deep denial and desperately needed help, not only through this stage, but to deal with his unresolved past. The counsellor told me that without counselling Frank would not move on but would continue to deteriorate emotionally.

I was deeply concerned for Frank's well-being and spent many hours discussing the pros and cons of counselling. Eventually he agreed to see the counsellor for just one month and only because I insisted. Not ideal but better than nothing, I thought. I didn't hear from Frank for some seven weeks, although up until then I had been speaking to him on a daily basis. He told me that he was seeing the counsellor regularly and had decided to continue with the counselling until the divorce was concluded. He still had a long way to go and, difficult as it was, it had made him realise how badly he needed someone with whom he could discuss his emotional turmoil. He was able to concentrate better at work and his relationship with his children was improving. It was important that he had found the right counsellor, someone in whom he could trust and confide, and who could help him.

If you do not get on with your counsellor, you should find another. For counselling to be successful, you need to feel that you can relate to your counsellor.

## Children

The parent who is left with both financial and emotional responsibility for the children naturally feels hatred at times against the parent who has left without so much as a backward glance, or so it seems. The parent with care is the one who, in addition to trying to adjust to the breakdown, must be available twenty-four hours a day, seven days a week for the children.

It is that parent who gets up at night and nurses a sick child, and then goes on to do a full day's work. It is that parent who cuddles the child when he or she is hurt or scared, comforts the child in the early hours of the morning when the child comes for reassurance, and wipes away the tears of the child who cries in anguish because he or she is missing the other parent.

It is that parent who has to cope alone with the tantrums and behavioural difficulties which may follow contact, who has to change sheets in the middle of the night when the child reverts to bedwetting because of the insecurity which can accompany separation or even contact visits. It is the parent with care who has to cope with a confused and defiant teenager.

And all the while, apparently unconcerned, the other parent parties and plays, seeing the children every so often, lavishing them with expensive gifts and extravagant outings. It is no wonder that you feel hatred towards the other, and want to punish your partner in whatever way you can. But stop and think first. What effect will your actions have on the children? Part of the reason why you react as you do may be from fear of letting the children go. It may be because you know that the children provide you with an element of power over your partner. You may also be scared of the outcome.

If the parent who has left was not interested in the children before the separation, you probably question the sincerity of their demand for contact after the separation. You may be scared for the children, instinctively wanting to protect them from the anticipated let-down and ultimate rejection. Try to look at the situation from an objective position, if possible. What if your partner wasn't interested in the children before the separation? Could it be because of the problems in the relationship and general unhappiness? Perhaps your partner was struggling to come to terms with some inner turmoil which he or she couldn't discuss with you?

Perhaps that parent really is indifferent towards the children and finds coping with young children whom he really does not know terribly well both difficult and tiresome. But he feels that, so as not to lose face, he must appear to be interested in the children and see them often, if only to wind you up or to impress the new woman. You hate him for his insincerity and for making demands for contact with the children that he will probably not be able or even want to meet.

Try to move forward rather than dwell on the past. With new beginnings, try to give each other the benefit of the doubt that perhaps the situation, at least in respect of the children, will be different now that you have separated. Allow the children to spend time with the other parent on a regular basis, irrespective of what the relationship was like pre-separation. They will all find their own way forward in their new relationship. It may well turn out that the interest is short-lived, lasting as long as the divorce proceedings. At least you will know that you have given the children every opportunity to develop the relationship.

If, however, the children are being hurt by failure to keep arrangements or by hostile behaviour, you will need to discuss the problems with your solicitor. This is very different from blocking contact because of your feelings alone. It is important for the children to know that they can always trust and rely on you – this will envelope them with the security they need to cope with the separation, divorce and beyond. What you want to avoid is your undiluted hatred for your former partner influencing and affecting the relationship which the children have with their other parent.

## The beginning of the end

Given time, you will become war weary. You will want to solve the problems more than you want to continue fighting. The aggression stirred by your hatred will start to feel like an enormous waste of energy. You may be willing to allow the children to spend a night, a weekend or even a week with the other parent, something previously not contemplated, and you will realise that, without noticing, you have moved on from the hatred stage.

Although this is an intense and frustrating stage, it also tends to be short. It is not a stage which is as outwardly vicious and damaging as the anger stage. Remember: this is the beginning of the end; you are entering the final lap and soon you will be free!

## Stage 6
# Grief

This stage means the end of the process is near. The instinct to fight ferociously for survival is followed by the need to mourn the loss of the life that was between you. The fight in you has gone, to be replaced by the will to survive. You need to rebuild your strength, your confidence and your life. Wounded and frail, or defiantly stronger from the experience, you want the certainty and finality that the divorce order will bring.

Look back at what you have been through, for it is only with hindsight that you are able to acknowledge how difficult it has been and how well you have coped. With anger, pain and hate behind you, emotionally exhausted from adjusting, coping and fighting, it is during this stage of grief that the remaining issues tend to be resolved.

You are both now more likely to be amenable to realistic negotiation and sensible compromise. You may be so fed up with it all that you cannot be bothered to argue any longer and wonder why you became so wound up about keeping the silver candlesticks which you didn't even want. You now want it finished – the sooner, the better. If you are unable to reach an agreement between you, you will have found your day or days in court expensive, stressful and generally unsatisfying as neither of you is likely to be pleased with the order imposed by the court.

Over this time, you have made adjustments and you both know what it is that you need, want and can expect. It is often at this stage that it all seems suddenly to click into place. Facing up to the end of a marriage gives you the chance to mourn its loss, an important part of the process. You may well feel apprehensive but, on the other hand, you will not be able to move on to the next stage of your life until the door of the present one is shut firmly behind you. If you leave it too long, you become lulled into what I call 'limboland': you are separated but living apart, neither married nor divorced, with no real impetus to change the situation. It is a false state, temporarily safe but unsatisfactory in the future, in which you can all too easily become stuck.

> Annie and Paul had been separated for five years. Neither of them took any steps to end the marriage, and the marital home, where Annie lived, remained in their joint names. Every now and then a half-hearted attempt would be made to divide the assets and deal with the divorce, but neither of them took any active steps. Annie always insisted that she wanted the only matrimonial asset, the house, to be transferred into her sole name. Nothing else would suffice. Paul was of the view that since he had always contributed towards the mortgage and the deposit, he should get half of the net proceeds when the house was sold.
>
> They grumbled about this on and off for years, with neither of them really pushing for finality. Then Paul met a new woman with whom he formed a serious relationship and had a child. Annie issued proceedings and took the matter to court. She knew, or it is hoped she had been advised, that her proposal was preposterous. No court would make an order in the terms she sought. It was only at the doors of court that she agreed to an equitable split so that Paul would retain an interest in their joint property, which was worth a substantial sum of money.
>
> They shared the grief; it was the end of their joint life. Even though they had been separated for seven years, until they took legal steps to end their marriage, they did not deal with the emotional stages. It was only after they had been separated a long time that they both acknowledged that their relationship was at an end, and experienced the consequent grief.

Give yourself the time that you need to grieve, and grieve each step as it happens, such as the pronouncement of the decree absolute, or the day your partner moves in with someone else. Each of these situations hurts and you need to deal with your feelings as they arise. It will help you to work through the stages of loss and adjustment. If you are the type of person who is not used to sharing emotions, you may find it difficult to cry and feel sorry for yourself without feeling weak or bad about it. It sometimes helps to write a letter that you would like to send your partner, even if you never intend to send it. Sometimes just putting your feelings down on paper is enough.

You may be scared, even at this late stage, to tell your partner how you really feel about him/her, the situation, the past and the future. This too is part of the healing process, and if you have the courage and the will, do it. It can help release pent-up feelings so that you no longer have to think 'if only' – if only I had said how I felt, if only I had done something else. This can help prevent bitterness which might otherwise never go away. If you have not said what you want to at this stage, it is not too late. And it may make all the difference. Counselling, too, can be a big help.

## Children

The grief which the children feel is quite different. They have not lost a parent as such but they have lost family life as they once knew it. Try to ensure that, in place of two warring parents, the children have two parents whose company they can enjoy without feelings of betrayal. They need to be constantly reassured that they can still love both parents equally.

They may feel grief beyond what you expected. Part of the reason may be that you, as a parent, have not allowed them to spend time with the other parent without continuing conflict. Children are generally very adaptable, but they need certainty and security.

If problems over the children continue, you may need to consider the following options:

- **Family counselling** where you both see trained counsellors with and without the children to help you identify the problems, consider the reasons for them and then work out a solution to resolve them. Timetables for contact can be prepared and follow-up sessions to review the position may be arranged.

- **Mediation** which I explain in Section Two. Mediation will only work if you are both committed to finding a solution and avoiding court intervention. Whatever is discussed in mediation is confidential. I often find that, in the early stages of separation, emotions are far too raw for a couple to contemplate mediation. However, it may be more suitable at a later stage. If there is a real or perceived imbalance of power between you and you feel threatened or bullied or too emotionally overwrought, do not feel compelled to go to mediation because your partner demands it. You do have a choice which you can exercise with care and not under pressure. No one can be forced to attend mediation – any attendance is voluntary.

• **Court proceedings**. This should always be the last option and is explained in Section Two.

## Time for grieving

Ensure that you take the time to grieve because this is a vital stage if you do want to start life afresh. You need to ensure that you give your marriage a proper ending. This stage can therefore take some time, and everyone should take as long as is necessary for them. You want to ensure that as and when you do form another relationship, you do not take with you all the baggage from this one.

## Stage 7
# Acceptance

Finally, after years of 'getting divorced', you are there! Your money is now your own, your life is now your own and, most important, you can now get on with your life. The final stage of acceptance is often an anticlimax. There are no great changes and often it is merely a formality. You will have accepted the deal, the divorce and the new life and may be well entrenched in a new lifestyle. If you can acknowledge each of these stages and understand that they are an integral part of the process, you will be more likely to be able to start afresh. One day you will realise that you seldom, if ever, think of the past and that you have moved on with your life.

Most of you will leave that chapter of your life behind you. Sadly, for some the acrimony continues long after the legalities have been concluded for the very reason that one or both of the parties is emotionally stuck at one of the previous stages. It is important that despite your ex-partner's behaviour you concentrate on your own well-being and do not get drawn back into destructive patterns of behaviour. If you start to feel drawn in emotionally, go back to your counsellor or make an appointment to see one. If it is a legal matter, pass it back to your solicitor who can deal with it.

Most relationships settle down after divorce. You will have established new routines, made new friends, and developed new interests. Concentrate on the present and future and try not to dwell on the past. There will be times when you still feel sad or angry, but that is to be expected.

## Children
If there are children, you and your ex-partner will still have to see each

other. If you really and truly cannot face each other by now, then don't. Make arrangements so that direct contact between you is avoided. In time you may find that you become friends or lose contact altogether. You cannot plan what the future will hold, so don't even try. Gain what you can from the experience and then do your very best to move on.

Insofar as the children are concerned, nothing is final. Maintenance can be reviewed either up or down if there is a change in circumstances or every couple of years to keep in line with inflation. If there is difficulty over contact with the children, or a specific issue needs to be resolved, either one of you can always return to court. If there is a Residence order in place, the person with residence cannot remove the children from the jurisdiction of the court for a period of more than a month without the other parent's consent or a court order. A child's surname cannot be changed without the other parent's consent or a court order.

Only time will tell how the children's relationship develops or diminishes with the other parent. Children generally adapt and get on with their lives. They have busy schedules and social calendars. With the number of divorces ever increasing, it is no longer unusual to come from a divorced family, though not surprisingly all children find it hard to cope with their parents' divorce, whatever their age. If they are confident about their continued contact with both parents, they are more likely to accept the situation. Rather than feeling they have lost a parent, they will have gained quality time with each parent. Sometimes the older the child, the more difficult it is for the child to adapt to the changes. How many times have you heard parents saying that they stayed together for so long 'because of the children'? They probably did stay together, truly believing it to be in the best interests of the children, but did they do their children a favour? Did the children know that this is how they felt? I hope not, for what a tremendous burden it places on a child.

Ben told me that his parents divorced when he was an adult. He was told that they had waited until all the children had grown up and left home before they divorced. How did that make him feel? Well, absolutely devastated. His entire childhood, which he had believed was happy, was swept away and replaced by a huge cavern of deception. Nothing was what he had believed and he was left emotionally stranded. His parents had thought that they were doing the right thing in staying together for the sake of the children. Were they able to maintain a picture of happy families and separate their dying feelings towards each other from those towards their children? Perhaps their real error was in telling their children why they had stayed together rather than simply informing them that they had made the decision to divorce.

I do not know the answers, but perhaps the lesson to be learned from this story is that parents should always be careful as to when, what and how they tell their children, whatever age they are, of the separation and ultimately the divorce. Even though as a parent you will want to do what is best for the children, sometimes you need to consider what is best for you. If you are settled and secure, you are more likely to provide a stable and secure environment for your children. Sometimes this may not be possible and divorce is the only option. This will then be the right decision for you and consequently for your children. Insofar as the children are concerned, any relevant change of circumstances should be reviewed and if necessary aired. Children with mum sometimes go to dad years later. Dad may disappear for years only to reappear – a potential minefield. But as always, if there are problems, discuss the options with your solicitor. You will then know what you can do and be able to take any necessary steps.

Accept that you may each have a different way of parenting, and neither way is right or wrong but merely different. Accept that your ex-partner does love the children and will look after them. Accept that eventually the children will find their own way with the changed relationship that they have with each of you. Accept that from time to time you will see each other and, for the sake of the children, you will have to be civil towards each other. School concerts, parents' evenings, sports days, weddings and family functions may always be uncomfortable. Somehow or other you will all adapt and find a way in which, while not necessarily grinning and bearing it, you will cope.

## Tying up loose ends

There will probably be quite a few loose ends to tie up, most of which will be dealt with by your solicitor. For example, a property may need to be transferred from joint names into a sole name, endowment policies may be surrendered, sold or assigned to one of you, and car ownership may be transferred, etc. All this takes time, but eventually it does get done.

Depending on your religion, you may need, in addition to a civil divorce, a religious divorce, for example, a Get, which is the Jewish divorce. Sometimes the religious aspect of divorce can take place before the civil one. Be sure that this is not overlooked as it is preferable to deal with all aspects at the same time. It can prove to be much more difficult at a future date, particularly if you lose contact with each other.

If you do not have a will, or if you only have one drafted whilst married, you need to make a new will. Divorce affects inheritance under a will. Where there is an existing will, any appointment of a former spouse as an executor or trustee is treated as omitted, and any gift to a former spouse lapses, unless there is a contrary intention in the will.

## Moving on

I was delighted last week to receive a call from Julia, a client who had gone through a long and particularly nasty divorce which included court battles over everything from the divorce itself to the children. Despite my constant reassurance, she never thought it would end and never truly believed that she would be able to move on. Nevertheless, when she felt low, we would talk about her dreams. She dreamt of having a cottage in the country where her children could walk to the local village school, where she would grow vegetables in the garden and look out over fields of flowers. She had always been a city girl and during her marriage lived a jet-set life of excessive spending and wild parties.

Her divorce was finalised eighteen months ago, she has her pretty cottage in the country and her dreams have come true. When she speaks, her voice is filled with happiness and hope. She has started dating and is studying towards a new profession. She also told me that, with the benefit of hindsight, she could see how and why she had reacted as she had during the divorce and how each and every one of the emotional stages which I had identified had been precisely how she had felt. Looking back, Julia was able to understand the whole experience and appreciate that even though it was excruciatingly difficult at the time, it was also essential that each stage was acknowledged and dealt with to enable her to move on to the next one.

Julia's story is not unique and there are many more like hers. But the key to it all is timing and, as I have said before, it will take as long as it takes and no one can predict how long that will be for you.

# Section Two:

## the legal process

# The legal process

Procedures, courts, rules, statutes – what do they mean? How do you find a way through the maze of law when you don't even know where or how to start? Does the very thought of finding out more fill you with horror? Does it make you want to dive under the duvet, hoping that it will all go away? By concentrating in this section on the financial element of separation and divorce, I hope to help you through the unknown territory of 'getting divorced' and, in doing so, to take some of the mystery out of the legal process and court procedures.

You may not yet be in the midst of a divorce, but it is on your mind and you need information. You may have choices which you don't feel ready to take. If undecided, bide your time if you can. Don't let friends or family pressurise you into taking steps until you are ready.

Whatever your reason for reading this book, whether you are at the beginning, the middle or nearing the end of a divorce, I hope that I can help you understand tactics that are used, advice given and the reasons why you are encouraged to respond in a particular way. When dealing with the financial element of a divorce, there are rules and procedures that must be followed. There are ways in which to manage a case to ensure that the outcome is to your advantage.

It is important that you have confidence in and a good working relationship with your solicitor, so that you can express your wishes and concerns. Your solicitor needs to be accessible and understanding, yet firm enough to guide you when you veer off the planned path. Trust your instincts and choose your legal advisers with care. You need to have sufficient confidence in your solicitor so that, even if you don't always agree with what is suggested, you will follow their advice in the knowledge that it has been given with your best interests at heart. Together you and your solicitor can establish a strong team to take you through this important phase of your life, one that will have long-term implications.

A solicitor can and should adopt an objective approach. Your solicitor can take an overview whereas, because you are so involved, you may not be able to see beyond the next day, let alone into the future when you will become an independent, single person again. And that objectivity is precisely what you need at a time when you may be confused, distressed and unsure in whatever you do.

Your solicitor won't make decisions for you, but can present and explain various options for you to consider so that you are better able to make decisions. A solicitor can provide a protective buffer between you and your partner until such time as you feel strong enough to fend for yourself, however long that may take.

Do not be afraid or embarrassed to seek counselling during separation and divorce. I am very much in favour of it, as I have seen the benefits that my clients have derived from it. You will need whatever support you can get and the fact that you are receiving counselling will not be held against you in any way. It is not the function of your solicitor to provide you with emotional support, but he or she can provide support in conjunction with a counsellor.

Eventually you will need to determine where you are going and you will want to ascertain how that can be achieved. If your wish is for an amicable resolution without court intervention, remember that a fair settlement is a settlement with which neither party is really satisfied – that is the spirit of compromise. In time you will find that you have developed the strength to get through it all. You will find that you are able to start afresh and look to new beginnings.

The successful separation of joint lives is never easy, but the secret of achieving separation with dignity and success lies within everyone's reach. It can be attained by reminding yourself throughout the process of the following points:

- Divorce is not a game so there can be no winners.
- To try to frustrate your partner is unsatisfying and counter-productive.

- Keep a diary of everything: it can be cathartic to write down your feelings, and if you need information, it will prove invaluable.
- Ask professionals questions until you understand.
- Do not act on impulse.
- Never act when under pressure.
- Do not be afraid to ask for help.

## The divorce

The emotional aspects of separation and divorce are covered in Section One. The divorce itself is a separate issue, the mechanics of which tend to be quite straightforward. Generally the divorce is the most simple aspect to resolve once the children and finances have been dealt with. Often the divorce itself is not initiated until an agreement has been reached in relation to the finances. It is then a quick and easy process, hence the term 'quickie divorce', although usually negotiations have been under way for many months or even years beforehand.

At present, the grounds for divorce are adultery, unreasonable behaviour, desertion, a two-year separation with consent or a five-year separation for which no consent is required. You do not need actual evidence of adultery, you just need to know about it and it must be admitted. Generally the admission takes the form of a statement contained in the Acknowledgement of Service, a standard form sent by the court together with the divorce petition. In answer to the question 'Do you admit the adultery alleged?', a reply of 'Yes' will suffice. In most cases, the third person is not named and the days of the private investigator providing photographs are long gone.

Unreasonable behaviour is any behaviour that you find unreasonable, and again no specific proof is required. Divorces seldom proceed on the basis of desertion. If you wish to proceed with a divorce on the grounds of a two-year separation, you need to have been separated for two years, although not necessarily living in separate households. However, if you remain in the same household, you must live separately, which means not eating meals together, not going out together, not doing washing for one another, and not watching television together. It is also essential that whoever is being sued for divorce consents to the divorce being granted after a two-year separation.

You do not receive compensation if you are the 'innocent' party and, by the same token, if you are sued for divorce you do not lose your entitlement to property nor are you denied rights to your children. All that it means is that the divorce can go through smoothly and as inexpensively as possible.

Provided that you have been married for a year, either of you can start divorce proceedings. You need to have your original marriage certificate and it does not matter where you married. A divorce petition will be prepared by your solicitor, and served (sent) through the post from the court direct to your partner or care of his or her solicitor. Your partner will need to complete and sign the Acknowledgement of Service confirming receipt of the petition. You can then apply to the court for a decree nisi to be pronounced. Six weeks and a day after pronouncement of the decree nisi, you can apply for the decree absolute which is the final decree. If you do not apply for the decree absolute, three months after the time when you could have applied for it your partner can do so.

The law is likely to change in the near future: a period of separation for reflection is all that will be required. It will not be necessary to establish any of the above grounds of divorce and the intention is to do away with the 'fault' element of divorce.

A divorce is seldom successfully defended, but it can be delayed. If you both co-operate, it can take four to five months from start to finish and no one need attend court. Remember that the divorce itself – not the deciding of how to divide the assets, which generally takes longer – can be dealt with separately. When the law changes, a minimum period of separation of a year will be necessary, rising to eighteen months if there are children. You will both be required to attend information sessions and no final decree of divorce will be granted until all issues in respect of the children and finances are resolved.

# The beginning

## What happens?

Tearful, angry or in despair, you may find yourself sitting alone wondering what you are doing, where your life is going and whether or not your relationship has reached its sell-by date. But what do you do? Where do you start? What happens if you see a lawyer? Is it truly the beginning of the end?

The children may be fighting and screaming, you may be sleep-deprived from stress and anxiety and your frayed nerves jangle so loudly you cannot hear yourself think. Even everyday decisions may be overwhelming. You look at your partner and silently wonder for how much longer you can both continue to torture and destroy each other, for how much longer you can pretend to play happy families while in reality you are tearing each other apart.

Perhaps the situation at home has been terrible for longer than you care to remember, but on occasions too numerous to recall your partner has told you that 'if you so much as contact a solicitor, you will regret it'. Do any of the following phrases or scenarios sound familiar?

**'If you see a solicitor, that will be the day when the financial tap will be turned off and all those unspoken evils will be revealed to all and sundry.'**

**'If you try to get a divorce, it will be defended and come what may you will get nothing, be nothing and have nothing.'**

**'If you try to get a divorce, you will lose the children and never see them again.'**

**'If you see a solicitor, all that they are after is your money and, before you know it, you will be caught in the midst of a full-scale battle, because that is what lawyers do – they make it worse! So agree with what is on offer because that is all you will get and keep the lawyers out of it.'**

What about the emotional blackmail when there are threats of suicide or self-harm if you take any steps to end the marriage? Or the situation in which children and family are exposed to emotional blackmail? At what point does it become so unbearable that you know you no longer have a choice but to take steps to separate? Are these thoughts and feelings ones that you have had over days, months or perhaps even years? Is there a pattern of behaviour in your relationship that manifests itself time and time again and then goes away for a while, only to return again and again... and again?

Nobody can tell you what is right and what you should do, although if friends and family know that you are experiencing difficulties, they will, with the best of intentions, give you their advice and opinions. It is a very personal decision, one that should not be taken lightly and one that generally only you can make. The golden rule is not to act in haste, on impulse or under emotional pressure. One day you will wake up knowing what you want to do. You will have decided whether the marriage is one that you feel is worth preserving, and you will have the strength to do something about it.

I have had many clients who believed, or so they say, that all was well until one day, out of the blue, their partner told them that it was all over. If you are in that position, consider honestly what it was really like. Was it so good or was it just easier to ignore or take a blinkered view about your differences and problems. Often it is much easier to turn a blind eye to building resentments or, perhaps because of your own insecurity, feel that you cannot ask for more or indeed for anything.

I don't have the answers but I am aware, as a family solicitor, that when I see clients and we start to go through the history of the relationship, the problems have usually been festering for a long time and the client has chosen not to acknowledge them because that was the easiest option. Even if you know that the relationship has become awful, it is still hard to face the 'D' word. Ask yourself if it really was as good as the moments you choose to remember; or if it was in fact rather awful most of the time and it was just a matter of biding your time until you were strong enough to make a decision.

I believe that in times of crisis you must use whatever support is available and appropriate. So many people balk at the thought of counselling, yet at this stage it is crucial, whether the relationship survives or not. If it does survive, you can prevent a repeat of the present crisis. If it does not, you will both know that, as a couple, you tried everything and it really is better to end the relationship.

What you don't want is to have more regrets than necessary. You don't want to look back one day and think, 'If only we had tried harder' or 'If only we had gone to counselling'. At times like this, you need to put your pride aside and do whatever feels right for you, and perhaps only time will tell what that is. No one can predict how long it will take and what I say to my clients, when asked that very question, is that it will take as long as it takes. Each case is different, your life, your personalities, your circumstances are individual and personal to you.

The golden rule is not to act in haste, on impulse or under emotional pressure. It is always hard to face up to the reality of the 'D' word; it is a major decision and should not be rushed. If in doubt, seek counselling, try again if you wish and take your time.

## Jurisdiction

If either you or your partner is not British, before you do anything else about a separation, you need first to consider whether the British courts have jurisdiction to consider your divorce. You also need to ascertain whether a separation or divorce might jeopardise your immigration status and right to remain in the country. Sometimes the right to remain depends on the marriage to your partner and issuing a divorce petition could result in deportation. If this is a potential problem, before you take any steps in respect of the divorce, take advice from an immigration lawyer.

It may also be appropriate to do some 'forum shopping', which means you should consider whether it would be preferable to issue proceedings in another country if the law in that country could achieve a better result for you. This may be particularly relevant in countries in which pre-nuptial agreements are recognised and valid in the event of marital breakdown, which is not the case in England and Wales. So chose your jurisdiction with care if you have the option.

To be able to divorce in this country, one of you must either be domiciled within the jurisdiction of England and Wales or have been habitually resident there for at least twelve months before the start of divorce proceedings.

## Questions about the matrimonial home

When caught in the midst of a relationship that is breaking down, the matrimonial home or the home in which you both live if you are not married is always one of the major assets to be considered. Many questions arise which may include the following:

- Is the property owned jointly?
- If so, is it held as joint tenants or tenants in common?
- If it is held solely in your partner's name, how can you protect your interest in the property?
- If there is a mortgage, is it an endowment, repayment or other type of mortgage?
- How do you decide who keeps the country house or the London apartment?
- Who keeps the council tenancy?

What happens if you want to separate? Who leaves the home? And if you leave, do you lose your interest in the property? Should the house be sold before you separate? At what stage should you seek legal advice? And what is the situation if you and your partner are not married but bought the house together? It is important that when you make a decision with such profound consequences, it is an informed decision. The way to ensure this is to know the facts and understand the legal implications rather than react negatively to an emotionally charged situation.

To a certain extent the way in which the matter is dealt with depends on your relationship with your partner. If you trust each other despite the breakdown and want the separation to be as civilised and amicable as possible, you can discuss your plans openly. You may both agree to sell the house and split the proceeds so that one or both of you can be rehoused.

The situation is different if there is an enormous amount of anger and mistrust. You need to be alert and aware, because you are both caught up with the emotions that accompany the breakdown of a relationship and you or your partner may behave or react in bizarre and bitter ways. In such a situation you need to ensure that your interests are protected.

Be aware of the following key points:

- If the property is solely in your partner's name and you do not trust him/her, you should register a caution under Section Four of the Matrimonial Homes Act or a Class F land charge. This will ensure that the property cannot be sold or further charged without your knowledge, pending legal proceedings or settlement negotiations. This should not be viewed as a hostile act but as action taken to protect your interest, and care should be taken not to use this in a vindictive way.

- If the atmosphere at home has become intolerable and one of you chooses to leave, that person does not lose any entitlement to a claim in the property. It does, however, introduce an element of calm to what may have become an intensely volatile situation.

- If you leave the home, take with you what is important because you may not get the opportunity to return for more if your partner becomes embittered and vengeful.

- If the property is to be sold, it is preferable that an overall settlement is reached in relation to division of assets rather than dealing with assets on a piecemeal basis.

- In resolving the finances, it is not necessary to liquidate all the assets. However, it is important to obtain updated valuations, preferably agreed, of all property and interests in property, so that an agreement can be negotiated as to who will keep what and what, if anything, will need to be sold.

- If you do not want to sell the matrimonial home until, for example, your youngest child completes full-time education, you can retain an interest in the property and be 'paid out' at an agreed date in the future.

- If you own a property with a partner as opposed to a spouse, your interest in the property is based strictly on property law. If you are joint tenants, your half share is recognised. If you are tenants in common, a declaration of trust may indicate your respective shares. Alternatively you may have made financial contributions towards the property, for example by putting down some or all of the money for the deposit, making payments on the mortgage or paying for improvements. These rights are now governed by the Trusts of Land and Appointment of Trustees Act 1996.

If you cannot agree between you who will leave if, for example, one of you wants to remain and buy out the other's interest, or if it is clear that the only option will be for the property to be sold and the proceeds be divided between you, but one of you will not agree to the sale, you may have no option but to make an application through the courts for the court to make a decision.

# Solicitors

## Finding a solicitor

What do you do first if you have the option of timing your moves at a pace that suits you? You think that your relationship may be at an end, but you are not certain. Perhaps you don't really want to discuss it with close family or friends. If you are in counselling, you will no doubt be discussing the issues with your counsellor.

Consulting a solicitor at the outset on a fact-finding exercise is sensible for two reasons:

1. To ascertain your rights and obligations to your partner and family;
2. To plan your strategy and decide what steps can and should be taken.

It does not mean that you will be frogmarched through a divorce come what may, but it does mean that when you are ready to make a decision, whatever that decision may be, it will be an informed one. Everyone who contemplates or faces separation and divorce has many questions to ask and correct answers can only be supplied by an experienced family lawyer. Don't be swayed by a friend who knows it all because he has been through a divorce! If you have had your appendix out, does it mean that you could take your friend's appendix out? Of course not and the same applies to divorce. No two cases are the same, so be wary of advice given with good intentions, which can be potentially dangerous.

In some cases, you may seek legal advice, consider the advice given and decide to struggle on with the relationship because financially you feel that divorcing would change your life too drastically. If you are in that position, I urge you to have couple counselling. If you plan to stay together, try to improve your relationship rather than carry on as before, which clearly was unsatisfactory. In other cases, you may seek legal advice, consider the advice and not make a final decision about ending the relationship until years later. But that visit to a solicitor will have helped you continue until you were ready to move on.

Solicitors really do not mind being consulted on a fact-finding exercise. That is one of their many functions: to provide information, to answer questions and, more importantly, to be a point of contact as and when further questions or problems arise. Some people find it reassuring to know that they have made contact with a solicitor so that if they run into difficulties they already have someone to call.

There is also no need to apologise to your solicitor if you choose not to proceed with a divorce, or halfway through the proceedings decide to halt the process. Don't be embarrassed by this: contrary to public belief, divorce lawyers generally do not encourage divorce. If there is any chance of saving your marriage, that should always be your first option.

By the same token, do not feel embarrassed about contacting your solicitor again if a reconciliation fails to work out as anticipated. If you find a solicitor you like, stay with that solicitor no matter how many times you stop and restart proceedings. Don't change solicitors because you fear that they may in some way judge you by your indecision in the early period of your separation, even if that period has lasted for years. They will not.

So how do you go about finding a solicitor, someone who is experienced in family law, who will advise you soundly and whom you can trust? It must be someone who will be understanding and sensitive to your uncertainties, needs and insecurities and who will be able to maintain calm. A solicitor must be conciliatory yet firm, able to deflect aggression from your partner without aggravating an already volatile situation. It should be someone on whom you can depend for the duration of the divorce, which can be anything from six to nine months to three years and more.

Most important of all, and I cannot stress this enough, is to ensure that the solicitor you choose is an experienced family solicitor. Don't go to an old family friend or your godfather's brother or the solicitor who did the conveyancing of Aunt Matilda's cottage way back when. Family law is a specialised area of law and having a solicitor who is not experienced in this area of law can only be to your detriment. Sensible negotiations may prove to be impossible, costs may be incurred unnecessarily, information may be refused and realistic proposals rejected because an inexperienced adviser doesn't know the rules and won't follow the procedures.

Ask around, if you have family or friends who have been through a divorce. Often personal recommendations can be a good starting point. If your friends have a solicitor whom they can recommend, make an appointment to meet him or her. If you are in counselling, your souncellor may recommend a solicitor. Another way is to contact the Solicitors' Family Law Association, which will be able to recommend experienced family solicitors in your area. Members of the Association must be experienced in family law and strive to abide by the Association's Code of Practice. Principally, the Code of Practice adopts a conciliatory approach to separation and divorce, encourages negotiation rather than litigation and discourages an aggressive adversarial approach. What all this means to you is that the divorce will be dealt with in as civilised a manner as possible, maintaining decorum and trying to achieve amicable resolutions to issues.

There is a great difference between aggression, which is always unnecessary, and being firm, which is often necessary. Avoid solicitors who are aggressive for the sake of it. Unharnessed aggression of a client, encouraged and vigorously supported by a solicitor, leads only to trouble, both emotional and financial. Ultimately it means that the only way in which the matter will be concluded is through the courts, which will increase hostility, costs and the time taken to reach a resolution. It can virtually destroy any prospect of an amicable resolution, let alone a reconciliation.

Bess came to see me when she had lost confidence in her solicitor. She had two small children and, when the baby was six months old, Gus had left her for another woman. He immediately sued Bess for a divorce based on the grounds of her unreasonable behaviour. On the advice of her solicitor, she defended the divorce on the grounds of her husband's unreasonable behaviour.

The case ground to a halt: it had become a 'defended divorce' and it would involve huge expense to allow it to continue on that basis. It was all so unnecessary. Had Gus received sensible legal advice, the divorce petition would not have been issued straight away, and when it was issued, it would have been better had it been done by agreement. Bess needed time to adjust to the shock and defending the divorce gave her time. They ended up having to withdraw both of their petitions and start again after a two-year period of separation.

It took almost that period of time for Bess to come to terms with Gus's audacity in leaving her for another woman and then suing her for divorce because of her alleged unreasonable behaviour. The damage to their relationship because of this aggressive and unnecessary start was irreparable and could so easily have been avoided. It impacted on the relationship which Gus had with the children and any sensible, experienced family solicitor could have predicted the outcome of such action and for that reason would not have pursued such a course.

The grounds for divorce have no bearing whatsoever on residence of the children or the division of finances. The grounds for divorce, be they adultery, unreasonable behaviour or a period of separation, are for the purpose of establishing a basis on which the divorce itself can proceed. The less acrimonious the divorce, the better it is for everyone. It is pointless to use the basis for the divorce as an opportunity to vent anger or any other emotion against your partner.

The intention of the Divorce Law Reform under way is to remove the element of 'fault' from the divorce process completely and the only ground for divorce will be a period of separation. But no law and no statute can ever remove the emotional elements which will always accompany a separation and/or divorce and which need to be acknowledged and dealt with in some way rather than dismissed as unimportant. Only time will tell in what way this will manifest itself once the element of 'fault' is in theory removed from the legal process.

A good choice of solicitor is a crucial starting point. Meet the solicitor of your choice and, if you are happy with your choice, stay with that solicitor for the duration of the case. The solicitor who starts a case will generally have a better grasp of all the issues than someone who takes it over from another solicitor. Generally, it is unwise to change solicitors midstream unless you have good reason to be dissatisfied. Question why you want to change solicitors – is your dissatisfaction justified or is it symptomatic of your general state of mind? Are you perhaps stuck in one of the emotional stages of divorce and therefore attacking all and sundry, including your legal adviser? If you have a gripe, discuss it with your solicitor. See if there is a constructive way forward. If you really have lost confidence in your solicitor, you may indeed need to change. However, if when you have been with solicitor number two for a while, you decide you are dissatisfied again, perhaps you need to look at yourself and try to ascertain where the real problem lies.

If you are in counselling, this is something you may consider discussing with your counsellor. If you are not in counselling, you should think about getting counselling. This leads on to the issue of how to find a suitable counsellor. Again, personal recommendation is generally a good starting point. Your solicitor or general practitioner may also be able to recommend a suitable relationship or individual counsellor.

Try not to be swayed by your partner's views about your solicitor. If your partner makes derogatory comments about your solicitor and his or her legal ability, you should ignore them. This is a fairly common ruse, an attempt to undermine your confidence in your legal adviser and therefore unsettle you.

Above all, do not enter into any negotiations with your partner or sign *anything* before you have taken legal advice, even though you may feel guilty about the separation and/or divorce, or bullied. It is more difficult to extricate yourself from a bad agreement than to start negotiations from scratch.

Ruth, a new client, came to see me. She was distracted and told me that she had been married to her husband for forty-two years and was very frightened of him. He was having an affair with another woman but refused to leave the matrimonial home.

She felt far too threatened by her husband to contemplate asking him to leave or seeking a court order to that effect, and she thought – wrongly – that she had insufficient grounds to do so. There had been no physical violence, but the emotional battering had been and continued to be harrowing. This can at times be even worse than physical abuse, and emotional abuse is recognised by the courts. Ruth clearly needed to be away from her husband, which would give her time to gather her wits and think more clearly. She was in no emotional state to make any decisions, let alone a major decision on which her future was to be based.

Under pressure, and without the benefit of any legal advice, Ruth and her husband sat around a table (with their grown-up children) and, without any input from Ruth who was too over-powered by them all, formulated an agreement which they all thought would be fair to Ruth. She felt bound by it and didn't know what to do. The agreement was formulated by people who knew nothing about the law. Her children had in fact done Ruth a great injustice, an injustice that she alone would have to live with. Although the agreement would not have stood up in court because there had been no financial disclosure and Ruth had not taken legal advice, she did not have the wherewithal to stand up to her husband. She also feared being seen by her children to renege on the agreement which she believed would alienate her from them.

Despite my advice that she see a counsellor, who could provide her with emotional support irrespective of what decisions she might ultimately make, she would not do so and I never heard from her again after I received a letter from her informing me that she had decided to do nothing.

## Prior agreement

Some couples manage over a period of time to negotiate the basis of a financial agreement that they are willing to accept. They feel that all they want the solicitor to do is to formalise it. A solicitor is under a professional obligation to advise you on whether or not the agreement is a fair one and, as I stressed earlier, it is generally unwise to reach an agreement without first obtaining legal advice. However, provided that the agreement appears to be a fair one, there is no reason why the input of a solicitor should not be minimal, limited to taking care of the legal formalities. This is only likely to be the situation in the case of short marriages, when there is little in the way of funds and no children.

Avoid signing anything, even casually, without first taking legal advice. For all you know, your partner may already have taken legal advice and not told you. By signing a document in these circumstances, you may place yourself in a disadvantageous position, one from which it may prove difficult and costly to disentangle you. Seek legal advice and, if necessary, do not tell your partner that you are doing so.

Even though you may be able to retract from part, if not all, of the agreement if you entered into it without the benefit of legal advice, don't allow your partner to pressurise you into signing anything unless you really understand the implications of the documents and still want to sign.

If, contrary to legal advice you receive, you still want the matter to be concluded on the basis that you negotiated with your partner, the solicitor can put that agreement into effect. However, it is likely that he or she will want you to sign a form of indemnity to the effect that, despite the advice given, you have entered into the agreement knowing and understanding that once it is made an order of court your ability to renegotiate the terms is severely limited.

Be that as it may, if you and your partner have been through your respective financial circumstances carefully and decide that you both want the matter concluded on the basis agreed between you, don't let a solicitor dissuade you when in your heart you know that what you have agreed is right for you. After all, you know your partner and you know if the information provided has been given openly.

By raising queries about the proposals you present, your solicitor is not trying to be obstructive; it is important for you to understand the principles behind family law and what you may be able to achieve if you persist with a further claim.

You may feel that it is more important to get on with your life without acrimony which, knowing your partner, you feel sure is what would happen if you tried to negotiate for more. But always remember that once an agreement is reached, it is highly unlikely that you will be able to return to court for more and that, if you settled in haste through fear or pressure, there is no turning back.

At the present time, the law provides no structure for the division of assets between couples who cohabit rather than marry. The 'common law wife' does not exist and, in these situations, division of assets is based entirely on strict property laws or, if you entered into a cohabitation agreement, in accordance with the terms of the agreement. Therefore if an asset is not in your name and you made no financial contribution towards it, you are not likely to have an interest in it.

## The first meeting

You may be at the very beginning of the process. You have the telephone number of a solicitor but do not know quite what you want to do with it. A crisis may erupt, leaving you with no choice but to call and make an appointment to see the solicitor. As a general rule of thumb, if in doubt, contact the solicitor, who will advise whether prompt and urgent attention is required or not. If there is no immediate crisis, hang on to that number so that if you eventually decide you do need a solicitor, you don't have to start your search all over again. If the problems pass, you may never use it.

When you feel that the time is right, make an appointment to meet the solicitor. You may make an appointment two or three times, cancelling each time before the meeting because at the last minute you do not feel quite ready. Do not worry about that, so long as you notify the solicitor that you wish to cancel the meeting. This happens fairly often before a first appointment. After all, it is rather a frightening admission to make to yourself that you are going to see a solicitor about your marriage and that this may be the first step towards divorce. It may be that you have never discussed the problems with anyone else and this is the first time that you will do so.

The first visit is often the most difficult one. You are experiencing the emotional turmoil which accompanies the heartache of separation and divorce. And there is no real way of easing the enormous pain that you will feel, particularly in the early days. Subsequent visits become easier, because by then you have met your solicitor and established a rapport that will continue for the duration of your case. Family solicitors are understanding, good at tea and sympathy, questioning you gently with the matrimonial tissues always close by.

You need not feel embarrassed if you cry or become forgetful or confused and this applies equally to both men and women. You may find it helpful if you make a list of questions that you want to ask the solicitor at the meeting so that these are at hand if you become distressed or if you forget some of them. You can then ensure that most of your immediate questions and concerns will be considered and discussed. Feel free to repeat questions or points you wish to make and take notes if it will help you.

## What happens next?

At the first meeting, you will discuss the overall handling of your case. Are you still living together or not? If you are, the last thing you want is to be sitting together at the breakfast table when a letter from your solicitor or the divorce petition arrives without warning through the post. Should you mention that you have seen a solicitor at all? And when should a letter be written? All this can be discussed at the first meeting. Very often, no decisions will be made and you will be left to digest what you have been told and contact your solicitor when you are ready to make the next move. Because most people find the first meeting stressful, the solicitor will usually send you a detailed letter explaining what was discussed. You will also receive a standard client care letter; under Law Society regulations this must set out details of the cost structure and complaints procedure.

You may be given an action list, which highlights information that you need to obtain before you next meet. If you wish to start divorce proceedings, you will need to give your solicitor your original marriage certificate. If you do not have it, you can either get another yourself or your solicitor will get one for you.

A solicitor will not mind you calling if you have genuine concerns. What can be exasperating is if you call constantly with trivia, or call repeatedly with the same questions either because you are not listening to the answers or because you are not being told what you want to hear.

Try to refrain from telephoning your solicitor frequently and unnecessarily as it runs up your costs and means that your solicitor can't get on with your case. Rather than sending pages of hand-written faxes and letters that may be difficult to read, try to send neatly typed notes dealing with as many points as possible at a time. This is much more helpful than sending many letters, each dealing with one point at a time.

You need to be realistic about what can be achieved by your solicitor. If your partner was difficult and unreasonable during the marriage, he or she is unlikely to be any different during the divorce. If anything, the aspects of your partner's personality that have caused you to separate are likely to worsen rather than improve during the divorce, so try not to expect otherwise.

You need a solicitor who is honest with you, one who will not paint an artificial picture and tell you only what you want to hear. This will lead to disappointment and dissatisfaction when reality sets in. Solicitors do not enjoy imparting bad news, but your solicitor owes it to you to give an honest appraisal of your case so that right from the beginning you are aware of the disadvantages as well as the advantages. Without this type of information, it is not possible for you to make informed decisions about your life and your future.

You want to avoid getting to the doors of the court and being told that you have no chance of achieving what you had hoped. By then it is too late and has cost too much. Your solicitor needs to advise you of the bottom line at the beginning and then reassess the situation realistically from time to time.

Even if you do not at first like the prospect of the potential outcome, in time you will adjust and get used to it. It is counter-productive to give you a false sense of security if you are wanting, for example, to have everything and more, when there is no way this could be achieved.

Although it is essential that you make the decisions in relation to your case, it is not helpful if the case is completely 'client driven': that is, the solicitor is unable to impose reason on an unreasonable client and does whatever the client demands, whether it is right or wrong. The result is that the case loses direction, leading nowhere fast but at a high price, and it tends to increase acrimony.

Trust your solicitor and take the advice given. Of course you are entitled to air your concerns and question the reasoning behind the advice being given if it is not immediately clear to you. But you also need to examine your motives if you are demanding that letters be written giving blow-by-blow accounts of incidents which may be occurring on a daily basis.

There are always two sides to every story and no one is more aware of that than a solicitor. Your solicitor is able to take an overview and not be side-tracked by the events and incidents that are driving you to distraction and which are part of the ongoing emotional turmoil of divorce. This aspect of divorce needs to be dealt with not through lawyers, but with the aid of counsellors.

I will come back to costs later in the book, but you should be aware that solicitors are paid on a time basis, so you are charged for every letter that they receive and write as well as every telephone call made and received. So it is no good telephoning five times a day, giving convoluted details of everything that has happened, and then complaining when you receive a large legal bill. To a certain extent the level of legal costs can be controlled by you.

# Costs

Costs will be discussed at the first meeting with your solicitor and often clients will ask for the hourly rate over the telephone before they even make the first appointment. If you feel that the solicitor's charging rate is too high for you, you can try to find someone who charges less. But beware: less is not necessarily best.

You may be eligible for Legal Aid and your eligibility will be assessed both on your financial circumstances and on the merits of the case. In family matters Legal Aid is generally granted if you fall within the set financial limit, assessed both on capital and disposable income, which is varied from time to time by the Legal Aid Board. You may qualify for Legal Aid but have to pay a monthly contribution to the Legal Aid Board, which continues for as long as the Legal Aid certificate remains in force. If you are on Income Support, you automatically qualify for Legal Aid, assuming the merits test is met.

It is important to remember that Legal Aid is not a gift but a loan. The Legal Aid Board in effect lends you the money to fund your case. Therefore if you recover or preserve anything, you have to pay the Legal Aid Board back for all the costs incurred. The fees will be taken direct from any money you receive and if you need capital to buy a property to rehouse yourself, the Legal Aid Board can take a charge over your property, called the 'Statutory Charge'. Interest is payable to the Legal Aid Board on the money owed and so the sooner you repay the money, the better. At present in matrimonial matters, the first £2,500 of monies recovered or preserved is exempt from the Statutory Charge.

Unfortunately, many people who have the benefit of Legal Aid seem to forget that it is a loan. Because they are not having to pay legal bills on a regular basis, they adopt an unreasonable approach and become embroiled in unnecessary and vitriolic litigation. Frequently the only asset is the matrimonial home and as a result of the huge legal costs incurred, the limited equity in the home is reduced to a level that is insufficient to re-house anyone.

If you have the benefit of Legal Aid, you are obliged to notify the Legal Aid Board of any changes in your financial circumstances. You are also obliged to be reasonable and therefore if someone with Legal Aid is persistently obstructive, unreasonable or rejects, without reason, sensible settlement proposals, the solicitor has a duty to report the matter to the Legal Aid Board. On investigation, the Legal Aid Board may revoke the Legal Aid Certificate if that person's behaviour amounts to an abuse of the Legal Aid fund and an inappropriate use of public funds.

If you apply for Legal Aid, your solicitor will provide you with the forms that need to be completed. Note that Legal Aid is not granted retrospectively and so you will not be covered by Legal Aid until you have a Legal Aid Certificate. You will either have to pay your solicitor privately or, if you are on Income Support, be given advice and assistance under the Green Form Scheme.

Litigation is very expensive and in all matrimonial disputes there is one fund of 'matrimonial assets'. This includes everything regardless of whether it was brought into the marriage by just one of you or acquired together, and whether it is in joint or separate names, it all falls into the same pot. The more costs that are incurred by either side, the less remains in the pot for division between you.

It is amazing how many people lose sight of this simple fact. Caught up in any one of the emotional stages of divorce, one or both of you may ignore the diminishing matrimonial pot in your crusade to punish your soon-to-be-ex-partner. Whatever the outcome, when you realise at the end the level of costs incurred, I wonder how many people really think that it was worth squandering on legal fees joint funds which could have been put to much better use for the family.

Sometimes you may be the one who is behaving correctly but you have a recalcitrant partner and there is no option but to keep on referring the matter to court. All you can hope is that your partner will eventually realise that the costs are not justified by the battle and then become more reasonable and co-operative. Unfortunately, you cannot force someone to be reasonable.

More times than I can recall, when in the midst of the emotional throes of divorce, one party or the other will tell me that they don't care what it costs, they would rather pay legal fees than pay their partner. That is of course until they start receiving hefty legal bills, which brings home the fact that thet would rather keep the money for the family than squander it on legal fees. Again this is intricately linked to the emotional stages they are experiencing and it is only as they work through the emotional stages, that they realise what they are doing and why.

## Costs at the end of the day

In matrimonial matters, there is no usual way in which costs are dealt with. If you are funding the case privately, your solicitor will require money on account at the beginning of the matter and will send you bills on a regular basis. If disbursements are to be incurred, such as counsel's fees or court fees, you will be expected to place your solicitor in funds in advance.

If the case is settled, which means that you are both able to reach an agreement without the case going to court, the costs will form part of the agreement. Usually there will be an agreement to the effect that either you both agree to pay your own costs or, in the case of a wealthier couple, the person who is in the healthier financial position may agree to pay part of or all the costs of the other.

But costs are always subject to negotiation. If one of you has adopted an unreasonable stance throughout with the result that costs were unavoidably increased, it cannot be considered unreasonable for the other to refuse to pay those costs. The costs were unnecessary and may have been incurred out of spite. So beware of fighting for the sake of your principles or for revenge, because at the end of the day you could find yourself having to foot a hefty legal bill.

I will deal with further implications on costs in the chapter on finances and explain how important it is to try to adopt a reasonable approach not only in terms of costs but also from an emotional point of view.

# First moves

Planning your opening moves may be more important than you realise. In order to retain a non-acrimonious forum, it is preferable that your partner knows that you have been to see a solicitor and that a letter will be written or that a divorce petition will be issued. The fewer surprises the better, unless there are real fears of violence or dissipation of assets, in which case no warning should be given.

> Lisa knew that Mark was to receive a large insurance pay-out and that, when he did receive it, he would immediately take the money and leave the country. She did not know the precise amount or when he would be paid, but she thought it was imminent. Mark refused to disclose any information about his finances and so it was necessary to make an application to court, without notice to him, for an order freezing the money until the matrimonial finances had been sorted out. He was furious. It could have been avoided if he had only accepted that he had no choice. Had he voluntarily given the information and undertaken not to remove any funds until the finances had been resolved within the divorce proceedings, there would have been no need for Lisa to approach the court for assistance. It all goes back to the emotional stages – he was angry and did not want her to get anything.

Each case must be considered individually. If you believe that your partner is siphoning off any funds, offshore or otherwise, to avoid having to pay you, urgent steps may have to be taken to preserve the matrimonial assets until the case is concluded.

If property is registered solely in the name of your partner, whom you believe may try to mortgage or sell it to obstruct your claims or perhaps to obtain security for personal or business debts, you need to protect your interest in the property by placing a Matrimonial Homes Act caution or a land charge on the property. This will ensure that you will be informed if your partner tries to take any of the steps mentioned.

Again, if you want to try to preserve a civil approach, your solicitor will write to your partner advising that, although a caution or charge has been lodged against the property, it should not be viewed as a hostile act but rather what is required to preserve the assets until the case is finished.

Feel free to ask your solicitor to let you have sight of draft letters to your partner or your partner's solicitor before they go out, in order to ensure that you are satisfied with the content and the tone. The first letter so often sets the general tone of the case and it is extremely important that your partner knows right from the outset that it is your wish that the matter be conducted on as amicable a basis as possible. Venomous letters may give you satisfaction in the short term, but in the long run they will do nothing but make you or your partner appear to be bitter and unreasonable and they should be avoided.

In your heart, because you may be so upset and angry, you do not want to appear or behave in a reasonable way because you want revenge. But be guided by your solicitor, for whatever you may feel inside, letters through solicitors are not the right conduit for your anger. Remember that if the case is not settled and goes to court, the letters may be placed in the bundle of documents for the judge to read, and you must always be seen to behave in the right way, to be reasonable and unaggressive. A sensible solicitor will not write letters that are inflammatory or aggressive, whatever you might want.

If the matter goes to court, you want to try to gain the sympathy of the court, if possible. This is only likely to be achieved if you adopt a reasonable approach at all times. Do not interpret this as meaning that you have to accept whatever happens or be timid. There are ways and means of achieving what you want and threats and aggression are not the answer.

Your solicitor will be quite happy to copy all correspondence to you and many do this as a matter of course. If you feel too fragile to cope with unexpected letters from your partner's solicitor, let your solicitor know. Rather than being afraid to open post, you can then go through the letters and documents together with your solicitor. This is often only a temporary phase; in time you will feel more able to cope with correspondence on your own.

It may sometimes be necessary, even before the first letter is written, to carry out preliminary enquiries into your partner's financial circumstances perhaps because you believe that your partner will not be open and honest. The more information you have, the better. Try to ascertain what companies, bank and building society accounts exist. Any information about investments, savings and insurance policies can also be helpful. Remember, however, that it is an offence to tamper with the possessions of others and this includes opening someone else's mail. So don't steam open letters and break open safes. The information should be easy to obtain without breaking the law.

In due course, it will be necessary to disclose the information gathered in this manner to your partner's solicitor. However, you can wait until your partner has given details in relation to finances known as 'disclosure'. If your partner has given disclosure, but fails to disclose information that you have, it will cast serious doubt on your partner's credibility. In the long run, this means that your partner is less likely to be believed in other matters and will have to work that much harder to retrieve position.

Always be alert! However clever either you or your partner think you are, when it comes to disclosure, honesty really is the best policy. Do not ever underestimate your partner, the solicitors or the judiciary. We have seen it all before, we have heard all the stories before and trying to mislead the court can backfire if you are caught and count against you.

> **Mandy was granted a substantially higher award than Selwyn had anticipated because the court did not accept that he had disclosed all his assets. An assumption was therefore made that he had substantial undisclosed funds and the bulk of what was disclosed went to Mandy. Selwyn was furious and had to pay all the legal costs for the privilege.**

If you are caught out in non-disclosure, you are likely to lose face with your partner, you will be disadvantaged if the case goes to court, and you may find that your solicitor is no longer able to represent you wholeheartedly. Your solicitor may even withdraw from the case and you will have to find new legal representation. So think very carefully before you try to mislead your partner and, in doing so, alienate your legal team and lose the court's sympathy.

Before your solicitor can even begin to ascertain what settlement will be appropriate, your general expenditure needs to be calculated, so start to keep details of your expenditure. You may find that you spend more than you think, so it is a useful, even necessary exercise to carry out. It will help you to calculate your future budget, a tighter one, for after divorce standards of living generally go down. As a rule, two families cannot live as well on the same amount of available income as they have done in a single household.

# The finances

## Criteria for consideration

With regard to the finances, before any settlement can be negotiated, you both need to give what is known as full and frank financial disclosure. Although there is a duty on both sides to negotiate, you will not be penalised for failing to do so if disclosure has not taken place. The final outcome is generally calculated on the basis of needs and ability to pay. I tend to take into account the criteria adopted by the court because, if the case is not settled, it is ultimately the court that will decide on the division of both capital and income.

The criteria adopted by the court are set out in Section 25 of the Matrimonial Causes Act 1973, which states that it shall be the duty of the court in deciding whether to exercise its powers to have regard to all the circumstances of the case, the first consideration being given to the welfare of any child of the family who has not attained the age of eighteen.

'The court shall in particular have regard to the following matters:

a) the income, earning capacity, property and other financial resources which each of the parties has or is likely to have in the foreseeable future including in the case of earning capacity, any increase in that capacity which it would in the opinion of the court be reasonable to expect a party to the marriage to take steps to acquire;

b) the financial needs, obligations and responsibilities which each of the parties has or is likely to have in the foreseeable future;

c) the standard of living enjoyed by the family before the breakdown of the marriage;

d) the age of each party of the marriage and the duration of the marriage;

e) either any physical or mental disability of either of the parties to the marriage;

f) the contributions which each of the parties has made or is likely in the foreseeable future to make to the welfare of the family including any contribution made by looking after the home or caring for the family;

g) the conduct of each of the parties if that conduct is such that it would be, in the opinion of the court, inequitable to disregard.'

The division of finances will be decided adopting these criteria and the reason for the breakdown of the marriage will have no bearing on the finances. Therefore if you are the Respondent (the person against whom a divorce petition has been issued or the person who is being sued for divorce), you will not be penalised in any way, either in respect of your rights with regard to your children or in respect of division of the matrimonial assets and income.

## What is financial disclosure?

As I mentioned earlier it is important to give full and frank financial disclosure, and this includes absolutely *everything*. Don't underestimate the legal experts and certainly not your partner. This may become a matter of survival between you and your partner and if you persist in trying to deceive the system, the system may well catch up with you. By refusing to play by the rules, you force your partner to take more radical steps to ensure a just outcome. Ultimately it really does not pay off!

Divorce lawyers, forensic and investigative accountants and judges are all trained and experienced in ascertaining the facts. It is not difficult to find the gaps and then ask the questions that you will have to answer and, in so doing, undermine your credibility. Failure to provide proper disclosure can damage your own case beyond repair. If you are not believed, the case will not be settled, and if it goes to court, the court is likely to draw adverse inferences against you.

So what information should you provide? Some of the information you need to gather is set out below:

1. Details of your income, which should include your last P60 and up-to-date payslips;

2. Details of any other benefits you receive from your employment, such as a private medical scheme and contribution towards your pension;

3. A schedule of all your bank accounts and bank statements for the past twelve months;

4. A schedule of all your building society accounts, details and statements for the past twelve months;

5. Details of all your pensions, which should include the following information from the companies:

   a) The current estimated transfer or surrender value;

   b) Details of any lump sum payment that is payable, together with the earliest date on which the lump sum payment could be made;

   c) What you anticipate receiving when you retire;

   d) Date of anticipated retirement;

   e) Widow's or dependents' pension;

6. Details of any other life policies or endowment policies that you hold;

7. Details of any shares, PEPs or other investments that you hold;

8. Details of credit or charge cards you hold, together or separately, with statements for the past year.

Make sure that you disclose all your interests in companies, trusts or businesses. If you have recently received an inheritance, a bonus or a gift or won the lottery, it all falls into the pot and must therefore be disclosed.

A frequent misconception is that, before an agreement can be reached, everything must be liquidated. This is not correct. The mere disclosure of an investment does not mean that you have to share it. What it does mean, however, is that if you particularly wish to retain something, your partner may receive something else of similar value.

By the same token, if your income is derived from your business, it will not be necessary to sell that business to raise money. Even though it may have a substantial value, it remains your source of income. And neither can your partner demand an equal share just because it is there. Your ability to produce a regular income will need to be preserved for the benefit of the family.

## Housing

One of the most important issues that needs to be considered when dividing the matrimonial assets is that of housing, particularly when there are children. Although the interests and welfare of children are of paramount importance, similar criteria apply when there is an elderly spouse who has been in a long marriage.

If possible, you should both be able to be rehoused. In reality this is not always possible and often the parent with day-to-day care of the children will receive the lion's share of the matrimonial home or sometimes all the proceeds of sale. It is possible to retain an interest in the property that can be realised at a later date, for example, when the youngest child completes full-time education. This is discussed in more detail in the chapter, Types of orders.

The matrimonial home may need to be sold and the mortgage and debts cleared, if possible. The parent with care will need to be rehoused in a property of a lesser value but mortgage-free or with a smaller, more manageable mortgage. The standard of living enjoyed while married tends to fall following divorce and this is reflected in the size and value of the new property.

Most people balk at the prospect of leaving or selling the matrimonial home. Sometimes it is the only option for couples who are locked in destructive conflict and who are incapable of living in the same property without destroying each other and often the children as well.

In these situations it is preferable for one of you to vacate the property voluntarily. In doing so that person does not lose any entitlement to a claim in the property, and separation will immediately alleviate the tension. The worst scenario occurs when neither of you will leave and you become prisoners in your own home.

If caught in this situation, particularly if there are children, you need to step back and look at what is happening to you, to your partner and to the children. Revenge and punishment may feel sweet at the time, but when couples become caught on the rollercoaster of destruction, it is easy to forget the great damage inflicted on those whom you claim to love as you try to destroy the one you now hate. If you decide to be the one to leave, talk it through with your solicitor before you do anything so that you can be advised on how best to go about it.

Whatever the circumstances, you will improve your case greatly by carrying out a careful housing exercise. If you are the husband, you will need to get particulars of suitable housing in a convenient and suitable location in which it will be argued on your behalf that your wife and children could live. If the children are to stay with you, the same exercise will apply.

It is no use presenting a local newspaper at court, having circled the cheapest and most unsuitable properties as being the properties you suggest for your family. You must be realistic and fair because in the long run that will count in your favour.

Furthermore, you must go and see the properties you select as being suitable. You can then give evidence to the effect that you have seen the properties and explain why you believe them to be suitable. This will help the court decide on a realistic level of housing which you can set if you have done the groundwork.

Similarly, if you are the parent with care of the children or the person who is financially more needy, you must also select half a dozen or so suitable properties, visit them and thereby provide the court with a clear indication of which properties are available in a particular area and within an appropriate price range.

Discuss the relevant price range of appropriate housing with your solicitor. The exercise will prove invaluable and may even help you, if you want, to demonstrate to the court that, in the circumstances, it is not worth moving and you should remain where you are. Whatever you want, you must actually go out and view those properties, however time-consuming and tedious it may appear at the time.

The matrimonial home will need to be valued. You can both agree on one joint valuer or each get independent valuers. Ultimately, if you get separate valuations and are unable to agree on the value, the court will take the average as the figure on which to work for the purposes of resolving the matter.

Most people tend to feel fairly territorial about their homes and so find it difficult to move. It is just as hard to sell when you each wish to retain the property for yourself. Unfortunately, however, few people actually manage to remain in the property after divorce because this is not financially viable. At some point you will both have to face up to the harsh reality of the changes that accompany separation and divorce and then move on with your life. Eventually either one or both of you will have to leave.

There are of course some who don't feel strongly about remaining in the matrimonial home. Some people find the prospect of a new home with new beginnings exciting, a symbol of the end of that relationship; others take longer to adjust to the changes and feel that it will be a while before they are able to move on financially or emotionally.

## What about pensions?

Be aware of changes in pension laws, although at present little is on offer for wives who have no pension of their own. At the moment all that the courts can do in relation to certain pensions is to carry out an earmarking exercise. This works as follows: when the husband reaches pensionable age, the wife will receive a previously agreed percentage of his pension. The wife loses this benefit, however, if she remarries.

Another option, a new concept, is pension splitting, which means that the pension will be split at the time of divorce in order to create pension provision for both parties from the one pension. If you think that this is an option you would like to consider, you need to ensure that you take proper financial advice with regard to investing a lump sum in a pension and know what the ultimate benefits will be.

The most usual way in which pensions are dealt with is for the person with no pension or with smaller pension rights than the other to be compensated by retaining a larger share of the matrimonial home or receiving a sum of money that can be invested in a pension.

Pension companies are able to provide information about your pension to your solicitor, notably the current transfer value, which is the value attributed to the pension for the purposes of the divorce. Other useful information relates to the amount of any lump sum payment, the date on which it can be taken and the amount that will be received on the date of retirement.

Older couples may consider whether it is financially worthwhile getting divorced at all. For example, if the husband has a good pension and the wife none, it may not be financially practical for the wife to seek a divorce, for if the husband dies and she has divorced him, she will lose her entitlement to a widow's pension, which could be substantial.

By the same token, in a case where the parties are nearing retirement age and have been married for a long time, the wife could quite legitimately defend a divorce brought by the husband on the basis that she would suffer grave financial hardship if a divorce was granted. She could lose her pension entitlement as well as a widow's pension in the event of her husband's death.

In this type of situation it may be appropriate to proceed for a judicial separation. This is seldom used, but it enables you to make financial claims on each other without actually getting divorced. If you do separate and need financial support or wish to deal formally with the capital and income arising from the marriage, the only way in which this can be done is either within divorce proceedings or within judicial separation proceedings, which are mainly used when one or both parties do not wish to be divorced on religious grounds.

## What is a Calderbank proposal?

In time, during the course of negotiations, you may find that you receive a 'Calderbank' proposal, or you may be advised to put forward such a proposal. The Calderbank proposal takes the form of a letter. It is a realistic and sensible basis for a settlement contained in a letter written on a 'without prejudice' basis. This means that it cannot be shown to the court until after an order has been made but before a decision has been taken regarding who will pay the costs. It will contain a carefully calculated offer made in an attempt to settle the financial issues and puts your partner at risk on costs if the matter goes to court and the court does not make an award higher than that offered by you.

The purpose of a Calderbank letter is twofold:

1. It enables settlement proposals to be explored even though the 'open' correspondence may indicate that neither side will yield. Because the Calderbank letter is written on a 'without prejudice' basis, the terms of the proposal, as was said earlier, will not be revealed to the court until the case is heard and a final decision is made. The District Judge who hears the case will have no idea what proposals have been made in an attempt to settle the matter before it goes to court.

2. If marked 'without prejudice save as to costs', it brings financial pressure to bear on your partner who, as I have said, could be ordered to pay your costs if the offer is not bettered.

If you do fail to beat the offer put forward in the Calderbank letter, you will be liable to pay the costs incurred from the date of the Calderbank letter to the date of the final order. This is because it was a reasonable offer which, had it been accepted, would have obviated the need for a trial.

So if you offered to settle the matter on the basis, say, that your partner retain 60% of the net equity from the matrimonial home and the court orders that your partner retain 65 per cent, you will have to pay the costs, because the court made an order providing more for your partner than you offered.

On the other hand, if you offered per cent of the net equity of the matrimonial home, and the court ordered that your partner should receive 75 per cent, your partner will not have beaten your offer and will be liable to pay the costs incurred from the date of the Calderbank letter to the date of the order.

Going to court carries its own uncertainties; there can be no guarantee of the outcome. You need to be constantly aware of the cost implications, which will diminish the matrimonial assets. A carefully drafted Calderbank proposal puts your partner at a very real risk of paying your costs. If you are the one putting forward the proposal, it is a good idea to put forward a fairly generous offer, as it will protect you in relation to future costs. The ultimate cost implications increase the pressure on your partner to consider the proposal seriously.

As previously indicated, if you have the benefit of Legal Aid, you are obliged to consider all realistic proposals. If you reject a proposal that is considered reasonable and realistic by your solicitor, he or she is obliged to notify the Legal Aid Board that you have failed to consider it. The Legal Aid Board may then discharge your Legal Aid certificate, which means that you no longer have Legal Aid and will have to fund further costs, which can be substantial, yourself.

The purpose of Financial Dispute Resolutions (FDR), is to see if a couple can reach an agreement without the case going to a full-blown trial. There is an obligation on both parties to negotiate and for proposals to be put forward in an attempt to settle the matter or at least narrow the issues.

> At a recent FDR, the husband had put forward a proposal which was nonsensical to say the least. After wiping the floor with him, the District Judge informed the husband in no uncertain terms that 'unrealistic offers *don't* count!'
> Unfortunately this particular husband was so caught up in the hatred stage that he was still a far way away from any sensible considerations.

I believe that timing is an important and often neglected aspect of settling any case, for until you are ready to let go, the case will not be settled. You cannot force agreement and sometimes a bit more time and patience is required to enable your partner to adapt and adjust to the changes. Given time, it may be that a settlement can be achieved, albeit not as quickly as you want but doubtless more cheaply than through a court trial.

# Procedures

If you have both given voluntary disclosure, which means that your solicitors have written to each other giving all relevant information about your finances with documents in support, you will soon be in a position to consider a proposal for settlement. But what if your partner refuses to give proper disclosure? The only way in which you can force your partner to do so is by making an application to court, which is both time-consuming and expensive.

There are two ways in which applications for finances are dealt with:

1. **The old format**, which is by way of filing affidavits of means, setting out all financial information, followed by questionnaires, after which the matter is listed for a trial if not settled.

2. **The Ancillary Relief Pilot Scheme**, the purpose of which is to streamline the procedure, get the parties to court more quickly and so move towards a settlement at an earlier date.

Under the Pilot Scheme, Form E affidavits covering finances are completed and sworn rather than the old-style narrative affidavits; all parties must attend the First Directions Appointment; questionnaires are still prepared and documents must be produced. There then follows a Financial Dispute Resolution (FDR), when all parties are required to attend court in the hope that, with everyone present, the matter can be settled. If this fails, the case is referred to trial. Your solicitor will be able to explain which procedures are applicable in the court you use.

If you reach an agreement but both of you want to wait for a period of separation to elapse so that divorce proceedings can be issued on the grounds of a two-year separation, you can enter into a Separation Agreement. This finalises the division of capital and income at the time of separation.

The jurisdiction of the court can never be ousted and agreements require the approval of the court. When divorce proceedings do get under way, a formal agreement will be drafted by your solicitor encompassing the terms contained in the Separation Agreement, which will be presented to the court for consideration and approval. Further, if there is a substantial material change of circumstances, either party can in theory reopen the agreement, although this is most unusual.

After the divorce proceedings are issued, the terms of any agreement are encompassed in 'Draft Minutes of Consent Order'. It can take some time from reaching an agreement in principle to finalising the agreed consent order.

The draft minutes of consent order cannot be presented to the court until the decree nisi has been given. The consent order, together with a Form M1 Statement of Information, will be submitted to court. The purpose of the Statement of Information is to provide the court with a snapshot view of the capital and income position of both parties, thereby enabling it to consider whether the agreement reached is fair and reasonable.

Generally the decree absolute is not applied for until there is an final order or agreement regarding the finances. This is particularly important in cases where the husband has substantial pensions, because in the event of the husband dying before the finances have been sorted out, the wife would lose the benefit of the widow's pension.

It is also crucial to be aware of what is known as the 'remarriage trap'. This means that if you have not made a formal application to the court in respect of your financial claims arising from the marriage, and you then remarry, you are barred from ever making a claim in the future. So if you want to get the divorce finalised but have not finalised the financial aspects and no formal application has been made to the court, you *must* notify your solicitor if you intend to remarry and you must do so *before* you remarry.

Your solicitor can then deal with the necessary paperwork to ensure that your interests are protected and a claim is made on your behalf. Because an earlier claim has been made, you can continue to negotiate a settlement or proceed through the court after you remarry. It is not necessary for financial matters to be concluded before remarriage, but it is essential that such a claim is before the court in advance of your remarriage.

# Courts and counsel

Attending court can be a daunting experience and, sadly, if your case is one in which you and your partner are unable to agree on anything, you may find yourself attending court many times. Most people, however, will never set foot in court. Each court is different and operates slightly differently. The two types of court situations that you are most likely to encounter are:

1. Hearings before a District Judge.
2. Hearings before a Judge.

To a lay person the differences are unclear. In essence, the Judge has greater power and jurisdiction and deals with matters of a more complex and weighty nature, and with matters such as residence of children, applications to remove or exclude one of you from the matrimonial home and complicated financial matters. District Judges can deal with divorces, hearings and trials in relation to the finances, direction appointments and matters related to the main hearing necessary to get the case to trial stage. Many hearings require attendance by solicitors only, although you may go along if you want to. Your solicitor will advise when it is necessary for you to attend court and you must then make sure that you do.

If you are expected to attend court but are unable to do so, you must notify your solicitor as soon as possible. It may be possible to adjourn the hearing if the other side agrees. If, however, they do not, unless you have a good reason, such as a genuine emergency, you are likely to be penalised on costs if the case has to be adjourned.

Expect to spend a fair amount of time sitting around in corridors as cases seldom start at the stated time. Take some bottles of water, drinks and snacks, if you wish, because generally the courts do not have good facilities.

Dress conservatively when you attend court as you want to try to make a good impression on the court. Wear smart but comfortable, conservative clothing and avoid very bright, colourful and heavily patterned designs, a lot of jewellery (especially if it jangles at the slightest movement) and wild hairstyles. Don't arrive in scruffy casual clothes and avoid wearing jeans. Other obvious points which spring to mind include not eating or drinking in court, not chewing gum, and not whispering loudly. If you need a drink, water is generally available on the tables.

## When to instruct counsel

You may ask why you need counsel at all. Why can't your solicitor attend before the District Judge? Your solicitor can appear at court before a District Judge but only before a Judge if he or she has a right of audience. There is a two-tier system comprising solicitors and barristers (also referred to as 'counsel'), each of whom fulfil different functions and roles. The solicitor is the person who will have the day-to-day care of your case, is the person to whom you will turn for immediate advice and information and who will generally prepare statements, affidavits and write letters. It is the solicitor who will negotiate for you and provide the buffer between you and your partner.

The barrister has no direct contact with you, the client. You cannot telephone a barrister or see one without your solicitor present. Your solicitor will select the barrister suitable for you and your case, will prepare the papers and send them to counsel. Counsel's role is generally to provide advice when all the information is to hand either on future tactics or on settlement. The barrister also spends a substantial amount of time in court arguing cases and therefore has the necessary expertise in this regard. Be guided by your solicitor as to when a barrister is appropriate, the key occasions being:

- To consider the proposal and perhaps to consider a counter proposal if an offer of settlement has come in from the other side;

- To formulate opening settlement proposals;

- To consider tactics and strategy before trial if the matter is clearly one which is not likely to settle;

- To attend hearings in order to argue your case before the Judge or District Judge;

Before any court hearing, your solicitor may suggest that you have a conference with the barrister. You will meet your solicitor at counsel's chambers, which is really only a grand name for counsel's office. It is always a good idea, costs and time permitting, to meet counsel before any court attendance. It gives you an opportunity to raise any questions that are bothering you and also to hear any points that counsel feels are relevant.

Generally you will meet your barrister before any court hearing and be able to establish a rapport with him/her. If for some reason you really do not get on, discuss this with your solicitor, who may be able, time permitting, to find another with whom you feel more comfortable.

When a barrister is instructed by a solicitor on your behalf, the solicitor becomes liable to pay the barrister's fees. Unless you have legal aid, therefore, you will be asked to place your solicitor in funds to cover the barrister's fees before these disbursements (as they are called) are incurred.

## In court

Hearings before a District Judge take place in the District Judge's court or, in some courts, a room, which is generally a large room with a long table. The District Judge sits at the head of the table and the parties and legal teams sit on opposite sides facing each other.

In some courts, the District Judge's clerk will sit in a corner of the room. Often one of the solicitors will have brought a trainee solicitor to court or a barrister will have brought a pupil along. They attend hearings so that they can gain experience in court. You may want to take a friend or relative along for moral support, but they will not be allowed into court because family proceedings are open only to the parties and their representatives.

Either your solicitor or counsel, if instructed, will speak to the District Judge. You do not speak to the District Judge direct, and if you have any comments, write them on a note pad and pass them to your solicitor.

In hearings which take place in a court room, the Judge or District Judge is seated elevated at the front of the court and the legal team and parties are seated down below facing the Judge. The barristers sit in the front row with solicitors and clients seated behind them.

District Judges and Judges tend to watch everyone very carefully, so it is essential that you remain calm and contained irrespective of how you are really feeling. Do not start huffing and puffing at statements with which you do not agree; do not start shaking your head vigorously, or wave your arms around, or even nod with great glee when you think a point has been made in your favour. In this situation, less is better, and the less indication you give of what you really feel, the better.

## Giving evidence

Only in cases where you are required to give oral evidence will you have the opportunity of having your say. You will be asked to sit at the end of the table if the hearing is before a District Judge and to swear an oath on the Bible or affirm, if you so prefer, that the evidence you are about to give is true. If the hearing is in a court room, you will go and sit in the witness box and be asked to take the same oath or affirmation.

At this point you will understand why it is so important to be open and honest, because when you are under cross examination by the other side's counsel or answering questions raised by the Judge, any discrepancies and inconsistencies in the information you have provided will be noted. Counsel are experienced in extracting the truth and demonstrating to the court the often obvious inferences which can be drawn if one party is not telling the truth.

If you cannot give plausible explanations of discrepancies, your credibility will be at stake and you run the risk of being penalised for your failure to provide reliable information when the order is made. If, for example, sums of money have disappeared and this is not explained in a believable way with documents in support, the court may take the view that the money still exists. Any award may therefore include the money that has supposedly been spent. Even worse, you may not be believed on other counts, so you will be at a disadvantage in every way.

When giving evidence, remember these three key points:

1. *Listen* carefully to the questions asked;
2. Answer *only* the questions asked;
3. If you don't understand a question, ask for it to be repeated.

Even though the lawyers will be asking the questions, direct your answers to the District Judge or Judge. Speak clearly and precisely and if you are nervous then say so. Everyone in court will understand, because giving evidence can be an unnerving experience. Refer to the District Judge as 'Sir' or 'Madam', and the Judge as 'Your Honour'.

Do not anticipate questions and do not jump to answer. If the answer you give is inadequate, you will be questioned further. Do not look to your solicitor for assistance because when you are up there in the witness box you are on your own. If everything you have to say is the truth, you have nothing to fear. If you have been less than truthful, the truth may well come out and at your peril. Be open and honest; otherwise do not seek or expect sympathy or support.

## Settlements at court

When you do need to attend court, you will usually meet your legal team an hour or half an hour before the hearing. This will give you an opportunity to discuss any last-minute issues and concerns. Your barrister will discuss the case with you, ascertain your views and give advice, but you make the final decision. Do not feel bullied or pressurised into making a decision and do be practical and sensible.

You may have heard of a case described as being settled 'at the doors of court'. What happens is that the barristers representing each of you talk to one another to see if there is a way in which a settlement can be negotiated. If successful, these talks result in a settlement at the doors of court and there is then no need for a trial.

The courtroom shuffle, as I call it, may continue for as long as necessary, you and your team at one end of the corridor, your soon-to-be ex and team at the other end. The barristers meet in the middle and discuss the issues and then return to their corners to update you on the discussions. You think about it, put forward a counter-proposal and your barrister goes back to speak to the other barrister.

It may all seem a bit strange, but this is often what happens when you get to court and very often cases can be settled in this way. There is always a risk that you may not do better if you go into court, and if you do not beat the proposals put forward you are at risk of paying not only your own costs, but an element of those of your partner. This tends to be a motivating factor in trying to reach a settlement at the doors of court.

If the case does settle, the solicitors and barristers will draw up an agreement or 'consent order'. It is important that you fully understand everything that is going on around you and understand the terms of the settlement. If in any doubt, ask questions until you do understand it all. It is your future that is being decided and the terms of the agreement will no doubt have long-lasting consequences on your life.

You must go through the agreement very carefully with your solicitor and counsel. The solicitors and counsel will go through it together until both sides are satisfied that it correctly reflects the agreement reached.

Everyone then goes into court and the barristers explain to the court that an agreement has been reached and, subject to the court's consideration, the court will approve the terms of the agreement. Because the agreement has been reached at such a late stage in the proceedings, you will not have saved much, if anything, in respect of legal costs, the work and preparation for the trial having already been done by the lawyers. The advantage of a settlement, however, is that neither of you need go through the difficult experience of giving evidence and the result is acceptable to both of you, which may not always be the case if a decision is imposed by the court.

# Types of orders

## During the divorce

Whilst all this is taking place, an interim arrangement needs to be made. You can reach an arrangement between you as to how bills will be paid, failing which an application can be made to court for maintenance pending suit. The court will make an order directing the level of maintenance to be paid until the matter is finalised.

As always, it is preferable to reach an agreement rather than have the court impose an order. If your partner has moved out, contact your local benefits agency in order to find out the benefits to which you may be entitled. If you are on Income Support, you will also be entitled to Housing Benefit, which will ensure that your mortgage interest or rent is paid. The Child Support Agency will become involved and make an assessment in respect of child maintenance.

It is more difficult when one of you is outside the scope of benefits, perhaps not eligible for Legal Aid, and your partner refuses to make a reasonable contribution towards the housekeeping and general expenses. Applications to court cost money, but in this situation you may simply have no choice but to make an application for interim maintenance to keep you going.

## Final orders

There is no set formula as to what the final outcome will be, but important factors to be taken into consideration by the court when reaching a decision include the length of the marriage, whether or not there are children and how the family can best be provided for.

So if the marriage is a short one with no children and both of you are young and self-sufficient, you would each hope to leave the marriage with what you brought into it. If there are children, the situation is completely different.

The interests and well-being of the children are of paramount importance and, wherever possible, the children will need to be rehoused. A young family with small children should aim to reach an agreement whereby the parent with day-to-day care of the children has somewhere to live, and maintenance is paid until at least the youngest child starts full-time education.

It may be that the only practical option is for the children and the parent with care to remain in the matrimonial home until the youngest child completes full-time education. The other partner can retain an interest in the property which will not be paid out until a later date. This is known as a 'Mesher Order'.

An alternative, called a 'Martin Order', entitles one partner to remain in the property with the interest of the other, an agreed figure of 25 per cent say, becoming payable only on the remarriage or death of the partner living there.

In other cases, it is appropriate that where there are sufficient funds to enable the assets to be divided, a 'clean break' should be achieved. This means that, following divorce, the parties will be financially independent of each other and neither of them will be able to make any further claims against the other.

To achieve this, capital will be divided so as to provide housing for the parent with care or the partner who is financially dependent on the other, and maintenance for that person will be capitalised: that is, the level of maintenance will be converted into a lump sum payable immediately or within a short period of time. This is done by using the Duxbery Tables, actuarial calculations that work out what capital sum of money will be needed so that, if properly invested, it will produce a lifetime income taking into account inflation and taxes.

Usually, the longer the marriage, the greater the obligation to maintain the other partner if one of you is not employed, is in receipt of a small income in relation to the other or is unable to become self-supporting. It is a matter of ascertaining precisely what is in the matrimonial pot and how it can best be divided.

The intention, if possible, is for both parties to be rehoused and have an income. While a wife at home with small children may achieve the lion's share of the capital, the husband will retain his income, save for the maintenance that he will have to pay. In time, he should be able to put down a deposit on another property and take out a mortgage based on his income or pension.

It is not possible to give examples of all the types of orders that are made and the above are just examples of what may occur. Each case must be considered on its own merits.

## Enforcement and/or variation

If an order has been made by the court, and this includes consent orders, breach of an order can be remedied by the court. There are numerous ways in which to take enforcement proceedings to remedy the breach of the court order but, as always, going to court results in further legal costs.

You may be in the position whereby you have no choice because your ex-partner is in breach of the court order and refuses to abide by the terms. Depending on the breach, the court can order the sale of a property or transfer of policies, and documents can even be signed on behalf of your ex if he or she refuses to execute documents pursuant to the terms of the court order – for example, if the matrimonial home is to be transferred from joint names into your sole name but your ex refuses to sign the transfer.

Maintenance can be subject to review and may be varied up or down depending on the circumstances. By agreement, the maintenance is often index-linked and varied automatically on an annual basis. An attachment of earnings order can deduct maintenance direct from employers and is a useful procedure if maintenance is either not paid or is not paid regularly.

If there are difficulties in relation to enforcement of the terms of the order or maintenance, discuss the appropriate remedy with your solicitor.

# Mediation

If discussing finances leads to rows, do not discuss the issue with your partner. You can either leave it to the solicitors or, if the situation settles down, you may want to consider mediation. Your solicitor will be able to recommend a mediator to you.

Mediation provides a safe impartial forum with independent mediators who try to help you reach an agreement. For it to work, however, you must both be committed to trying to reach a resolution. It should not be used as a means by which to bully your partner into whatever it is that you want or to delay matters.

There are a number of models for mediation and you will be able to choose the one that suits you best. You can attend mediation to discuss the children only or the finances, or you can opt for all-issues mediation, in which you can deal with everything from the separation and divorce to the finances.

Mediators have to be independent and impartial. So even if your solicitor is a mediator, you will need to use another mediator for mediation. You can continue to consult your solicitor during the process of mediation and many clients see their solicitor before or after mediation sessions.

The mediators will not enter into correspondence or telephone conversations with either of you. All communications should be confined to the mediation sessions and whatever is discussed is done so in the presence of both of you.

Generally it takes between four and six sessions to formulate an agreement. If little progress has been made by then, the mediators may suggest that the mediation process be terminated and the matter continue through solicitors. In this situation, although the mediation has not resulted in a settlement, it may have helped to narrow some of the issues.

If you reach an agreement, the mediators will prepare a 'proposal', which incorporates the terms of the agreement reached. You then take the proposal to your solicitor, who will deal with the legal and procedural formalities.

# Final reminders

All over – or is it?

Having made your way through the minefield of emotions and legal procedures, one day, believe it or not, you will find that it is over. At least the legal side will be over. By concluding the formal legal proceedings, you will be able emotionally to close the door behind you and venture into the world to start again or to continue to build the new life that you have already begun to make for yourself.

Some of you may find yourselves drawn into conflict again with an ex-spouse, but in most cases your ex will also be able to let go and move on, leaving you, and what was your shared life, behind.

If you have children, from time to time you will be brought together and you will learn how to cope with these difficult situations. It is far better for the children to have a good relationship with each of you and not be drawn into any conflict that may exist. It is never easy, but do your best.

Time in divorce tends to be a great healer.

Jonathan had an awful divorce. His wife fought about everything, wanted everything and delayed everything for as long as possible to prolong his remarriage. His children were never allowed to stay with him or to meet his new partner. At times, Jonathan told me that he wanted to walk away as it was far too traumatic, quite unbearable. But it did end and they did all move on. Jonathan told me recently that his ex-wife had remarried and had had a new baby. He too had remarried, they had built an extension to the house and, best of all for him, he saw his children whenever and as often as they wanted. In this case, they have all moved on and, in so doing, they each have new lives.

And so can you.

# Conclusion

Cast your mind back to what probably seems now like a lifetime ago when your thoughts were consumed by indecision about the status of your relationship. Can you remember how you felt or what you did, or does it seem too long ago? So much has happened since then that it is difficult to recall it all. No doubt you have changed beyond recognition, not only to yourself but also to others.

Do you remember all the time and energy that was spent during the early days in simply trying to get through each moment, let alone each day? Often paralysed by your fear of the unknown, did your thoughts revolve around and around the same questions? You constantly asked yourself whether or not you should separate, get a divorce or see a solicitor and if you did, how would you survive?

And now? Now it has passed, you have surpassed your own expectations and coped. What you may never have thought possible has happened. This may not be what you wanted. With hindsight some of the difficulties may have been a result of your reluctance to let it happen. Perhaps you really did have to be dragged kicking and screaming through the process (figuratively speaking, one hopes) because, for so many reasons, you were resistant to the changes and just didn't want it to happen at all.

You may have felt devastated by your lack of choice in the decision, your partner having presented you with a *fait accompli* and, other than delay the process, there was little else you could do. And that in itself was unbelievably difficult because of the diverse emotions which you experienced.

No one ever said it would be easy, but perhaps no one told you either that it would be quite so hard. And yet, despite the anger, the pain and the suffering, you discovered your own inner strength which is what buoyed you along when you thought you simply could not go on much longer. But you did, and to your own credit you have started again, a bit older and a whole lot wiser.

From time to time, you may still experience pangs of one emotion or another – you cannot simply obliterate a chapter of your life. It is not easy, but in time the episodes become less frequent and more insignificant.

Eventually, without being conscious of what you are doing, you will have started again. You will have made new friends, acquired new skills, developed new interests and found that you are no longer the person that you were when you were together with your ex. There is a new you or perhaps the you that had disappeared under the control of your ex. Perhaps as one part of a couple you lost your identity as an individual, and it is that which has resurfaced.

It is only now, when it is over, that you can look back at what has happened and hope to understand why it happened. And even if you can't understand it all, by now you may feel that too much has changed and it really doesn't matter any more. You may still feel at times that you would like to have achieved some form of revenge – two stories spring to mind which I hope will bring you solace.

Sandra was left by her husband with four small children. He left her with no contact address and substantial debts. Although established in her own career, she was unable to manage on her own and had no option but to give up her job and go onto State benefits. What had previously been a fulfilling and satisfying life became a difficult one, both emotionally and financially. From being an independent career woman and mother she became a single mother dependent on the State. In her hours of despair, particularly bad at three o'clock in the morning when she was unable to sleep, she thought of the many ways in which she could seek revenge and punish her husband for what he had done to her. But she didn't do anything because she was too busy trying to survive and keep the family afloat.

That was twelve years ago. Since then she has remarried, to a man who treats her far better than her first husband ever did. She has another child by her new husband and has gone back to work. Once again she is a working mother, content and secure with her new life. And she shared with me her words of wisdom. She believes that the very best and most satisfying revenge one can take on an ex is to do well, to get on with your life and to be happy.

When her husband left her, he believed that she would not manage without him. She could not change a light bulb, let alone do anything more complicated around the house. But she triumphed over adversity and, in so doing, she felt she had achieved the ultimate revenge. She retained her self-respect and dignity and remains a proud woman, one who realises that you cannot take your life for granted, but if it doesn't work out as planned, it is possible to start again.

Her husband Rick eventually remarried too, but not the woman for whom he left her. Although he had no contact with his children for a long time, after some years they resumed contact. For each of them, life has carried on, albeit on completely different paths from the one on which they set out together when they first married. With hindsight, Sandra is now immensely relieved that she did not do the things she used to think of doing in order to punish Rick.

Then there is Rowena, posh, well-educated, wealthy and glamorous. When Peter left her, he told her it was because of her unreasonable behaviour. She believed he left her for another woman, but whatever the real reason, they both behaved appallingly before, during and after the separation. Neither would see sense, everything was a challenge in which neither would give an inch and they were both unable to control their emotions or reactions to situations.

The result was that their divorce was an acrimonious one in which they both squandered thousands and thousands of pounds in legal fees. Their two small children were witness to endless screaming and shouting, and were often present when they chose to seek revenge against each other.

Once when Rowena found Peter's car outside his girlfriend's house (he persistently denied having a girlfriend at all), she drove in a rage to the nearest DIY store, even though she had her children in the car with her, and bought two large cans of paint, one of which she poured over Peter's brand new BMW and with the other painted 'You F**** Bitch' in huge letters along the girlfriend's front wall. Peter could not resist retaliating, so he drove around to her house, let down all her tyres, pulled up all her flowers and littered her lawn with garbage.

And so it went on and on. But to what end? Although the legal side is over, the battle continues, each of them constantly trying to outdo the other. Neither has formed a satisfying new relationship, although both have been involved with a stream of suitors who soon tire of the pettiness that consumes them both. The children are nervous and distressed and are in therapy.

Rowena and Peter themselves refuse to get therapy, each blaming the other and believing that it is the other who is in need of therapy. If they would only seek counselling, it could help them to let go and then move on. Neither of them is able to acknowledge what they are doing or the part which they played in the breakdown of the marriage.

Both of them have always had their own way and for once life has not worked out as planned, and they simply don't know and don't want to know how to cope. It is quite apparent that they are both stuck emotionally and without the benefit of counselling they will never be able to progress.

Try not to let that happen to you – if you still feel stuck, do something about it. It is never too late and no one can do it for you.

My intention in writing this book was to give you hope and sustain you through the process. I am sure that you thought you would not experience the emotions that were set out and that the final stage of acceptance seemed an eternity away. It was – but you reached it nevertheless. And if you are still not quite there, rest assured that, with assistance, you too will get there – just keep going.

I will end as I began. For those who are not quite there yet, let your daily chant to yourself be:

> **No matter how hard it all seems**
> **No matter how long it all takes**
>   **Be strong,**
>     **have hope,**
>       **it does all end.**

# Appendix:
# Legal procedure in Children Act applications

In this section, I deal with Children Act applications in the private sector only. Depending on whether or not your divorce has started, an application to court will either be made within the divorce proceedings or under a free-standing Children Act application. Your solicitor will advise you.

Both the parents' and children's rights are governed by the Children Act of 1989. Section 1(1) of the Act provides that 'in determining any question with respect to the child's upbringing, the child's welfare is the court's paramount consideration'. Section 1(5) provides that 'no court shall make an order unless it considers that doing so would be better for the child than making no order at all'.

What this means is that if parents are able to reach agreement in respect of residence (with whom the child shall live), and contact (how often the other parent will see the child), the court will not become involved. Therefore it is only if you are both unable to reach an arrangement over the children that you will need to consult a solicitor and consider making one or more of the following applications:

- **Residence Order.** With whom shall the children live?

- **Contact Order.** How often will the children see the absent parent?

- **Prohibited Steps Order.** That one or both parents be prohibited from behaving in a certain way, doing something, or taking the children away.

- **Specific Issue Order.** A specific issue such as schooling or removing the child from the jurisdiction for a holiday is decided upon.

The Application for an Order Form under the Children Act is a simple one which needs to be completed and signed by you. At the time a divorce petition is issued, a Statement of Arrangements for the Children will also need to be completed and signed. This sets out details of the children, their schooling, where they live, if they have any special needs, etc. Make sure that if there is anything on which you do not agree, it is set out clearly on the form. Your solicitor will help you complete the forms.

Having completed the Application for an Order Form, a fee will need to be paid and your solicitor will 'issue' the application. 'Issue' means that the application is sent to the court, the court stamps the application and allocates a case number. If the matter is urgent, an early court date may be fixed for the first appointment at court before a District Judge. Otherwise it may be some weeks before a date is allocated.

In extremely urgent matters, an application may be made 'ex parte'. This means that the application is made to court and an order is made without giving notice to your partner that you are going to court.

An early return date, usually a few days later, is fixed so that all the papers can be served on your partner. He or she will then have an opportunity to accept or argue the terms of the order that has been made. Matters are only dealt with on an ex parte basis if they are extremely urgent and the child is at risk.

The first appointment at court will generally be a conciliation appointment. The father and mother will attend at court at a given time, together with their solicitors if they so wish. A conciliation officer will be available at court to discuss the issues and difficulties with the parents, both together and separately. In some courts children over the age of nine years are expected to attend court so that the child can also talk to the conciliation officer and express his or her views.

Children are not allowed in court and, as many courts have no facilities for children, it is a good idea to take along a friend or family member who can sit with the child whilst the parents are in court. You would be wise also to take drinks, some snacks, and books or a game for the child, as a fair part of the day may be spent in the court corridors.

Explain to the child that the conciliation officer is there to try to help mum and dad reach an agreement over arrangements. They need not be frightened, and as the conciliation officers work all the time with children, they are aware that it is a new and daunting experience for them.

At the conciliation appointment no one need feel under pressure to agree to what is proposed. Your solicitor will be available to advise you, although generally will not go into the meeting with you. Make sure that you fully understand the proceedings, and if in doubt ask your solicitor to explain anything which you do not understand before any decisions are made.

If an agreement is reached at the conciliation appointment the District Judge, before whom the case is listed, can make an order in the terms agreed. The matter may also be re-listed for a further conciliation appointment in, say, six months' time to review the arrangements and see if they are in fact working.

If no agreement has been reached, the District Judge will set a timetable for the case. This usually includes:

- Each party filing a statement setting out the circumstances of the case from their perspective;

- The Court Welfare Officer being directed to see the parties and the children and to prepare a report;

- After the Court Welfare Officer has completed the report, the matter being listed for a full hearing before a different Judge some months later.

Generally it will not be necessary for the child to attend court for the final hearing. It is very important that you co-operate fully with the Court Welfare Officer, on whose report the judge may ultimately depend in making a final judgement.

Any time between the start of the case and the final hearing, you can try through solicitors, mediators or counsellors to resolve the problems without further intervention of the court. Sometimes this is not possible, however, and the only possible way forward is through the courts.

Insofar as children are concerned, nothing is final. Maintenance can always be reviewed either up or down if there is a change of circumstances;

or reviewed every couple of years to keep up with inflation. If the Child Support Agency is involved, maintenance should be reviewed on a regular basis. If not, you may wish to approach the Child Support Agency for them to make an assessment for payment of maintenance.

Those issues which fall outside the jurisdiction of the Child Support Agency will still need to be dealt with either by way of agreement or through the courts, the main issues being:

- If the absent parent earns in excess of the upper limit set down by the Child Support Agency;

- If one of the parents lives outside the jurisdiction of the court, i.e. outside the United Kingdom;

- If school fees are required to be paid.

Another point to note is that, save where a child is a ward of court or is the subject of a residence order, the leave of the court is not required to remove the child permanently from the United Kingdom where those who have parental responsibility are in agreement. Where, however, the matter is in dispute, the issue may be determined by the court as a specific issue.

Unmarried fathers do not, as of right, have 'parental responsibility' over the child. This can be acquired by the mother and father entering into a Parental Responsibility Agreement which is lodged at court. If no agreement is reached, an application can be made to court by the father for the court to determine the issue of parental responsibility. It is preferable if this can be resolved by way of agreement.

Parental responsibility provides legal recognition of the fact that the father is the father of the child. Should there be problems at a later stage in relation to the child, the father would then be entitled to make applications under the Children Act as set out above.

# Useful contacts

**Solicitors Family Law Association (SFLA)**
PO Box 302
Orpington
Kent BR6 8QX
Tel: 01689 85 0227
Fax: 01689 85 5833

**Family Division Courts**
First Avenue House
42–49 High Holborn
London, WC1 V6HA
Tel: 0171 936 6000.

**UK College of Mediators**
PO Box 3067
London WC1H 9SP
*The College sets standards for family mediators.*

**Family Mediators Association (FMA)**
PO Box 2028
Hove. East Sussex BN3 3HU
Tel: 01273 74 7750

## National Family Mediation (NFM)

9 Tavistock Place
London WC1H 9SN
Tel: 0171 383 5993
Fax: 0171 383 5994

## Family Mediation Scotland

127 Rose Street
South Lane
Edinburgh EH2 4BB
Tel: 0131 220 1610
Fax: 0131 220 6895

## Mediators Institute Ireland

13 Royal Terrace West
Dun Laoghaire
Dublin
Ireland
Tel: 00 353 1 661 8488
Fax: 00 353 1 661 8706

## Relate

Herbert Gray College
Little Church Street
Rugby CV21 3AP
Tel: 01788 573 241
Fax: 01788 535 007

## Institute of Family Therapy

24–32 Stephenson Way
London NW1 2HX
Tel: 0171 391 9150

## Jewish Marriage Council

23 Ravenshurst Avenue
London NW4 4EE
Tel: 0181 203 6311
Tel: 9345 581 999 (Helpline)

## Asian Family Counselling Service

74 The Avenue
London WC13 8LB
Tel: 0181 997 5749

## Catholic Marriage Care

Clitheroe House
1 Blythe Mews
Blythe Road
London W14 0NW
Tel: 0171 371 1341

## Gingerbread

16–17 Clerkenwell Close
London EC1R 0AA
Tel: 0171 336 8184
*Support for single parents.*

## Families Need Fathers

134 Curtain Road
London EC2A 3AR
Tel: 0171 613 5060
Tel:0181 886 0970 (Helpline)
*Advice and support for parents following separation.*

### Reunite

PO Box 4
London WC1X 3DX
Tel: 0171 404 8356
*Provides help and support for parents whose children have been abducted.*

### Stepfamily (National Stepfamily Association)

Chapel House
18 Hatton Place
London EC1N 8RU
Tel: 0171 209 2460
Tel: 0990 168 388(Helpline)

### British Association of Counselling (BAC)

1 Regent Place
Rugby
Warwickshire CV21 2PJ
Tel: 01788 57 8328
*Maintains a register of approved counsellors.*

### Young Minds

102–108 Clerkenwell Road
London EC1M 5SA
Tel: 0171 336 8445
Tel: 0345 62 6376 (Helpline)
*Provides information and advice for parents concerning children.*

### One Plus One

12 Burlington Street
London W1X 1FF
Tel: 0171 734 2020
*Provides literature obtained from research into the causes of relationship breakdown.*

# index